'This is a wonderfully written and important book ... ...,... in understanding the philosophy and psychology of Nietzsche and its application to the human condition. Dr. Clemente, in a very clearly written book, shows the importance and relevance of Nietzsche to contemporary depth psychology and how Nietzsche anticipates much of the depth psychology that came later. This book is fascinating and incredibly relevant for anyone interested in a deeper understanding of the human condition.'

David Olsen, PhD, LCSW, LMFT, *executive director,*
Samaritan Counseling Center of the Capital District

'Clemente offers readers a fascinating series of reflections on some of Nietzsche's most important and personal ideas, including his life-long quest to find a path to happiness and even joy in a life marked by great suffering. Retaining the conversational flow of the discussions out of which it springs, this work remains highly accessible to those new to Nietzsche's ideas while also penetrating deeply into their meaning and value for life. Clemente's guidance through the thick but fruitful forest of Nietzsche's thought will prove useful not only for professionals in the field of psychology and social work, but also for anyone seeking meaning and happiness while honestly confronting the full weight of life's trauma and suffering.'

Thomas P Miles, *author of Kierkegaard and*
Nietzsche on the Best Way of Life

POSTTRAUMATIC JOY

Posttraumatic Joy presents the major themes and ideas of Nietzsche's corpus from a continental and psychoanalytic perspective with a particular bent toward how they might illuminate ways of coping with and living beyond trauma and suffering. Through a series of transcribed and edited lectures—originally delivered as a part of the "Nietzsche for Clinicians" workshop run through the Center for Psychological Humanities and Ethics at Boston College—this work traces the genesis of such fundamental psychoanalytic concepts as repression, the death drive, and the Oedipus complex to the works of one of philosophy's most audacious and original thinkers. Reading Nietzsche not as a philosopher in the traditional sense, but as a proto-psychoanalyst, a precursor to Freud and Lacan, this work explores his understanding of the origins of morality, the value of sublimation, the movement from mourning to melancholia—or, in Nietzsche's terms, from trauma to tragedy—and the possibility of a life lived in affirmation and self-overcoming.

This interdisciplinary book will be of interest to scholars and practitioners whose work intersects with continental philosophy and theoretical and philosophy psychology. This includes any psychotherapist, social worker, psychoanalyst, or pastoral counselor with an interest in understanding the deep psychological philosophy of one of history's greatest thinkers.

Matthew Clemente is a husband and father. He is a Research Fellow in the Center for Psychological Humanities and Ethics at Boston College and the Assistant Editor of the *Journal for Continental Philosophy of Religion*. His latest book, *Technology and Its Discontents* (coauthored with David Goodman), is forthcoming from Oxford University Press.

Andrew J. Zeppa is a graduate student in philosophy at Boston College.

Advances in Theoretical and Philosophical Psychology
Series Foreword
Series Editor: Brent D. Slife

Psychologists need to face the facts. Their commitment to empiricism for answering disciplinary questions does not prevent pivotal questions from arising that cannot be evaluated exclusively through empirical methods, hence the title of this series: *Advances in Theoretical and Philosophical Psychology*. For example, such moral questions as "What is the nature of a good life?" are crucial to psychotherapists but are not answerable through empirical methods alone. And what of these methods? Many have worried that our current psychological means of investigation are not adequate for fully understanding the person (e.g. Gantt & Williams, 2018; Schiff, 2019). How do we address this concern through empirical methods without running headlong into the dilemma of methods investigating themselves? Such questions are in some sense philosophical, to be sure, but the discipline of psychology cannot advance even its own empirical agenda without addressing questions like these in defensible ways.

How then should the discipline of psychology deal with such distinctly theoretical and philosophical questions? We could leave the answers exclusively to professional philosophy, but this option would mean that the conceptual foundations of the discipline, including the conceptual framework of empiricism itself, are left to scholars who are *outside* the discipline. As undoubtedly helpful as philosophy are and will be, this situation would mean that the people doing the actual psychological work, psychologists themselves, are divorced from the people who formulate and re-formulate the conceptual foundations of that work. This division of labor would not seem to serve the long-term viability of the discipline.

Instead, the founders of psychology—scholars such as Wundt, Freud, and James—recognized the importance of psychology in formulating their own foundations. These parents of psychology not only did their own theorizing, in cooperation with many other disciplines; they also realized the significance of psychology continuously *re*-examining these theories and philosophies. This re-examination process allowed for the people most directly involved in and knowledgeable about the discipline to be the ones to decide *what* changes were needed, and *how* such changes would best be implemented. This book series is dedicated to that task, the examining and re-examining of psychology's foundations.

Suffering and Psychology
Frank C. Richardson

References

Gantt, E., & Williams, R. (2018). *On hijacking science: Exploring the nature and consequences of overreach in psychology*. London: Routledge.

Schiff, B. (2019). *Situating qualitative methods in psychological science*. London: Routledge.

Posttraumatic Joy

A Seminar on Nietzsche's
Tragicomic Philosophy of Life

Matthew Clemente
Edited with Introduction by
Andrew J. Zeppa

Routledge
Taylor & Francis Group

LONDON AND NEW YORK

First published 2023
by Routledge
4 Park Square, Milton Park, Abingdon, Oxon OX14 4RN

and by Routledge
605 Third Avenue, New York, NY 10158

Routledge is an imprint of the Taylor & Francis Group, an informa business

© 2023 Matthew Clemente

The right of Matthew Clemente to be identified as author of this
work has been asserted in accordance with sections 77 and 78 of
the Copyright, Designs and Patents Act 1988.

British Library Cataloguing-in-Publication Data
A catalogue record for this book is available from the British Library

ISBN: 978-1-032-39196-0 (hbk)
ISBN: 978-1-032-39197-7 (pbk)
ISBN: 978-1-003-34879-5 (ebk)

DOI: 10.4324/9781003348795

Typeset in Bembo
by MPS Limited, Dehradun

For Tracy
Thou, sun, art half as happy as we.

So little cause for carolings
Of such ecstatic sound
Was written on terrestrial things
Afar or nigh around,
That I could think there trembled through
His happy good-night air
Some blessed Hope, whereof he knew
And I was unaware.
~ Thomas Hardy, "The Darkling Thrush"

Contents

Foreword—Who Is the Fool? by Richmond Rugg   x

Editor's Introduction—by Andrew J. Zeppa   xiii

Author's Preface   xv

List of Abbreviations   xviii

1   First Meeting, 01/27/2022—Mourning and
Melancholia: From Trauma to *The Birth of Tragedy*   1

2   Second Meeting, 02/24/2022—The Value of Values:
The Psychology of Morals   15

3   Third Meeting, 03/31/2022—Bad Conscience:
Whence the Super-Ego?   28

4   Fourth Meeting, 04/28/2022—God Is Dead:
Living in the Absence of the Father   41

5   Fifth Meeting, 05/26/2022—Our Virtue:
An Honest Look at Suffering and Joy   55

Appendix—Two Eulogies   68

Index   71

Foreword

Who Is the Fool?

Castigat ridendo mores.
~ Erasmus

The author of that playful little adage once wrote in a letter to his friend and fellow merrymaker Thomas More—this, of course, before More lost his head—that he should like those who take offense at the frivolity of his writing to reflect upon the fact that such jocularity is not of his own accord, but a trait inherited from a long line of eminent authors. Plato understood the comic. He died with a copy of *The Clouds* under his pillow. Seneca knew how to laugh. He showed the powerful what pumpkins they really are. Even the God of Erasmus—author of this world if we are to believe that imbecilic ox from Aquino—cannot help but to put his tongue out at readers now and again, though perhaps it takes Shakespeare to reveal just how many jokes are hidden in holy writ. Yes, it takes a Shakespeare or, at very least, one who aspires to be a Shakespeare. And there's no doubt that Herr Nietzsche possessed such outsized ambitions. Consider the title of his autophilosophy, *Ecce Homo*. Behold the man beholding himself and finding there … a *better* Jesus? Better how? Not more moral, that much is certain. But perhaps more mirthful? More artistic? More subtle? More refined? One capable of counseling the daughters of Jerusalem, "Weep not for me. Laugh at yourselves"? After all, how pretentious are our lamentations? How pitiable, how joyless, how thoroughly *unchristian*?

That questions like these arise from any genuine engagement with Nietzsche's philosophy hints at a secret wisdom masked just beneath the surface of the text. Had he not expressed a "terrible fear that one day I will be pronounced *holy*," one might reasonably accuse him of angling for martyrdom, attempting to evangelize the baptized by offering them a scapegoat onto which they could project the venom and stupidity of their hearts. Indeed, the rejoinder that follows his protestation against any future attempts at canonization suggests as much: "I do not want to be a holy man;

sooner even a buffoon.— Perhaps I am a buffoon.—" (EH, "Why I am a Destiny," §1). Perhaps. And if so, what a marvelous accomplishment such clowning would be. For, the third metamorphosis of Zarathustra is to become again like the child (Z, "On the Three Metamorphoses") and, as Shakespeare's king in fool's garbs tells Lear, "Fool" is the title "thou wast born with" (Act 1, Scene 4). To return, then, to the gaiety of youth is no mean thing. It is, rather, the greatest wisdom—the wisdom of folly. And, as both Solomon and Paul attest, folly is the only wisdom capable of confronting an asinine world (see, Proverbs 26:5; 1 Corinthians 3:19).

Riffing on this defense of divine simplicity, my friend and colleague Jean-Luc Beauchard writes, "To speak frivolously about serious matters is a corrective in an age that is serious about frivolities" (MM, p. 34). Etch that in stone, drive it to Lützen, and fix it atop Nietzsche's crypt. Who, after all, is more hilarious than him? *Hilarious*? The master of suspicion? The enemy of reason, morality, and truth? The trumpeter of the death of God? I'm afraid other words come more readily to mind. And yet, if we are to take Nietzsche seriously, we'll have to entertain his proposition that philosophy is a *gay* science. We'll have to consider whether, in spite of its start as "a long tragedy," philosophy is not actually an epic comedy with every philosopher playing the part of the raving Quixote (BGE, 2, §25). We'll have to ask what it would mean to be a Socrates who knows how to dance (BT, §15).

Three decades ago, when I was conducting research for a book on Greek tragedy, I asked myself why Nietzsche chose not to write a companion piece to *Birth*, one which introduced the third art impulse made manifest by the sublimity of Greek culture: the Momusian spirit of divine mockery and jest. In the intervening years, I have settled upon a theory, one which the writing of this Foreword has convinced me is true. It is my contention that Nietzsche not only identified and articulated the impulse deified by Momus; he embodied it. Nietzsche's corpus cannot be read as anything but caprice. Yet it is caprice exalted to the heights of Mount Olympus, a sort of celestial nose-pulling and mischief-making that ascends higher than any philosophical system ever could. Presenting the most serious matters in a boisterous *allegrissimo*, he dances past danger like a swordsman laughing as he parries and prepares to strike. To miss this is to misunderstand *The Birth of Comedy*—that is, philosophy itself. What Nietzsche teaches us is that to conceal oneself in one's writing (see, BGE, 9, §289), to make of philosophy an elaborate game (BGE, 6, §205), a joke reserved only for the few (BGE, 2, §29), is to return the ancient love of wisdom to its foolish beginnings and invite it too to partake in that third metamorphosis, a perpetual childhood, an eternal recurrence of the new.

But who today is willing to take up so monumental a task? Who bears Nietzsche's mantle and carries it forward? That the book you now hold proposes a way through trauma to tragedy represents, in my mind, a first step. It opens the door, if only a crack. Still, what is needed is for someone to come along and kick that door in. Oh, how one longs to see so bold and decisive a figure. How one *lives* to see him! ("Grant me from time to time—if there are divine goddesses in the realm beyond good and evil—grant me the sight, but *one* glance of something perfect, wholly achieved, happy, mighty, triumphant, something still capable of arousing fear! Of a man who justifies *man*, of a complementary and redeeming lucky hit on the part of man for the sake of which one may still *believe in man!*" (GM, 2, §12)). Is such a one out there? Could such a one still exist? All we can do is await his arrival, hoping that Nietzsche's Momusian philosophy is a herald of things to come, a prelude to a philosophy of the future that may, *deo volente*, be realized somewhere in someone even in our present age …

Richmond Rugg

Editor's Introduction

To the poet, to the philosopher, to the saint, all things are friendly and sacred, all events profitable, all days holy, all men divine.

~ Ralph Waldo Emerson, *Essays*

Nota bene: The text herein was adapted from a seminar on Nietzsche's philosophy aimed primarily at practicing psychoanalysts, psychotherapists, and social workers. The course, entitled "Nietzsche for Clinicians: Learning to Live Between Trauma and Tragedy," was offered through the Center for Psychological Humanities and Ethics at Boston College in the spring semester of 2022. The assigned readings that form the basis of discussion for each meeting are as follows: (1) "Attempt at a Self-Criticism" and Sections 1–5 from *The Birth of Tragedy*; (2) Preface and First Essay from *On the Genealogy of Morals*; (3) Second Essay from *On the Genealogy of Morals*; (4) Section 125 from Book Three of *The Gay Science* and "Zarathustra's Prologue" from *Thus Spoke Zarathustra*; (5) *Beyond Good and Evil*, with a focus on the Preface and Parts One, "On the Prejudices of philosophy," and Two, "The Free Spirit." Questions and comments from the course participants are included with their permission and have been edited for clarity and concision.

❖

With perhaps the exception of audiobooks, which have increased recently in popularity, we don't often experience auditory versions of the written word. And we experience the reverse—written versions of the vocalized word—even less so. If you think this is inconsequential, simply listen to a podcast or talk radio show and then listen to an audiobook version of any well-written work of fiction or nonfiction. The latter will strike you as stiff and lifeless compared to the former. This is because the written word is crafted spatially, formally, and for posterity, while the spoken word—with its fluidity, informality, variable pitch and volume, and temporality—is meant to be heard in real-time. Simply put, they are different modes of communication that demand different aesthetic considerations.

Given the premise of this book, the challenge was to maintain the conversational, informal fluidity of the seminar while addressing the practical needs for organization into discrete spatial and logical units, and for the clarity and coherence that entails. Whenever possible, we have endeavored to preserve the spirit of the seminar. As a result, readers may encounter the occasional repetition or reframing of key points, the candid use of personal examples, interjections, informal language, cattywampus sentence structures, at least one instance of crass vocabulary, and even the odd intentional grammatical error, without all of which something critical is lost.

❖

My first serious encounter with Nietzsche's philosophy, to what I'm sure would be his chagrin, came by way of Wagner. During a certain chapter of my life, it was the music of *Tristan und Isolde* endlessly on repeat—the undulating angst of the prelude, the intoxicating mystique of Brangäne's warning, the tragic yet ecstatic climax of Isolde's *Liebestod*—that consoled me, motivated me, lulled me to sleep, and brought me to tears. What was it about this music, and the story it conveys, that so deeply affected me, a century-and-a-half after it did so for Nietzsche? The question is as much an aesthetic one as it is a psychological one, and I shall not be able to answer it here. Nevertheless, I will suggest that what Nietzsche may have recognized in Wagner was an open-endedness—a fascination with contradiction, an embrace of tension, a willingness to thrust forward a question and leave it hanging mid-air, even while the dust settles below.

From Socrates to Wittgenstein, the practice of philosophy as therapy has a long history of proponents. But philosophy, like therapy, will not yield any concrete answers. And like psychotropic medications, it comes with the risk of side effects: Taking philosophy may result in vertigo—a dizzying cycling between moments of clarity and disillusionment, divine order and utter chaos, meaning and meaninglessness. What, then, can be said for the value of philosophy as therapy?

What follows can be considered as a meditation on this question, though it is but one interpretation of the complex philosophical writings of one particular, and particularly great, thinker in history. Nietzsche's philosophy demands vitality. It is lived out creatively and amplified by new renditions. Therefore, as the editor of this volume, it is my hope that readers will feel they are a part of the conversation. I invite you to read with us, think with us, despair with us, hope with us, and most importantly, laugh with us.

Andrew J. Zeppa
Boston, Massachusetts
All Hallows' Eve
October 31, 2022

Author's Preface

I was on the phone with my closest friend. We were talking, as we invariably do, about writing. All writing, I was saying, is an attempt to memorialize the past. What the author desires most is permanence. Life is ephemeral. It is always going away. The illusion that sustains the author and keeps him writing is that he knows how to fix that problem. Plato, I was saying, has this habit of referring to authors as "wizards." Cervantes too. There is something magical about writing, something religious. It's as if you can stop time and reverse it, take a memory, so long dead, and bring it back to life again. You can salvage what's been lost, commemorate the past and carry it forward into the future, take what was and turn it into what will be forevermore. The Egyptians, I was saying, left us a work called *The Immortality of Writers*. It argues that, instead of leaving progeny of flesh and blood, authors create immortal ones. Plato puts something similar in the mouth of Diotima. What author hasn't felt that? I asked. What author doesn't dream of it?

I heard a beep. There was a call on the other line, a number I did not recognize. I ignored it, went on talking, smitten with the grandeur of my words. The same number beeped in again. I asked Will to hold. My wife had taken our three children with her to her doctor's appointment and I wanted to make sure it didn't have anything to do with that. I clicked over and found out that it did. I spoke with her obstetrician. I clicked back to Will and ended our call. I dropped my phone on the floor and began screaming.

I screamed the entire drive to the OB's office. It was like nothing I had ever experienced before. I could hear myself screaming, see myself screaming, but I could not stop myself from screaming. I thought that if any of the neighbors saw me, they would think I was insane. I thought maybe I was insane. What rational person can witness himself the way I was witnessing myself—see himself from without—and be incapable of intervening, utterly helpless to stop? If that isn't madness, what is?

As I pulled into the parking lot of the doctor's office, I began to regain my composure. I parked, went in, walked past the receptionist, found my wife, kissed her, talked to the doctor, explained to my kids—ages 5, 4, and 2—why they had not heard their brother's heartbeat, walked them out and put them in the car, buckled their seatbelts, drove them to my parents' house, left them with my mother, drove home, and drank more whiskey than is advisable in the middle of the afternoon. With the exception of my analyst, I have not told this story to anyone, have not wanted to return to the pain of that afternoon, the horror of losing my son and losing control of myself.

These events took place about six months before the seminar you are about to read commenced. Our son Anthony, who at nearly 20 weeks gestation was what doctor's call an "early stillborn," died on June 16th, 2021. In a life that has seen its share of misery and death, losing him was my greatest shock, the most traumatic rupture. Nothing could have prepared me for it. There was no reason to expect it. And for a long time, I did not know if I would recover.

Nietzsche opens the reissue of his *The Birth of Tragedy* with a preface he titles "An Attempt at Self-Criticism." In it, he goes on to praise the work (and its author) with the kind of hubris we expect from a self-styled Übermensch. Self-criticism, he seems to suggest, always conceals a hidden self-satisfaction, the narcissism of one who loves himself too dearly and watches himself too close. Chesterton makes the point that the humble man is liable to talk too much. Reservation is a sign of conceit, and so too is self-critique. Nietzsche, of course, knows this and in his typical provocative fashion, challenges us to acknowledge it as well. He does so without explaining. He illustrates the point. To parrot a trite truism authors know well, he shows without telling. He respects his reader.

Appended to this work, you will find two eulogies, the first given at Anthony's funeral, the second offered eight months later—on the morning of the second meeting of this seminar—at the funeral for my daughter Victoria with whom my wife was pregnant for a mere 12 weeks, whose heartbeat I had only just seen four days before. I have been criticized—rightly, I think—for being too autobiographical in my work. Scholarship is meant to be impersonal. Disinterest is the scholar's craft. But I hope it will be clear that I view such naval gazing as a weakness, not a strength. This book, titled *Posttraumatic Joy*, is meant to offer a path through trauma, a way beyond suffering that sees in suffering the necessary precondition for joy.

Have I found joy? Am I happy? At moments, yes. But the need to memorialize the past, to give testimony, to bear witness—the authorly desire to play God and resurrect what's been lost—seems to suggest a hidden melancholia, a dissatisfaction with the way things are, a fantasy about *what might have been*. As I read back over that last sentence, I recall that the word *martyr* means "one who bears witness" and am consoled by a line from Nietzsche. How does joy, he asks, relate to trauma? It bursts forth like a rose among brambles "even as the rapturous vision of the tortured martyr arises from his suffering" (BT, §3). I am no martyr, not in the true sense, nor am meant to be. But I have suffered, as have we all.

And I've come to believe that the goal in this life is to bear witness to that suffering and hope beyond hope that joy is still possible, that happiness—or, better yet, love—can be found in the very teeth of anguish. It's a beautiful thought. And the wisdom of Nietzsche and the love of those around me almost make me believe it—

Matthew Clemente
Boston College
All Saints Day
November 1, 2022

Abbreviations

Texts by Nietzsche

BGE *Beyond Good and Evil*, trans. Walter Kaufmann (New York, NY: Vintage, 1989)

BT *The Birth of Tragedy*, trans. Walter Kaufmann (New York, NY: Vintage, 1967)

EH *Ecce Homo*, trans. Walter Kaufmann (New York, NY: Vintage, 1989)

GM *On the Genealogy of Morals*, trans. Walter Kaufmann (New York, NY: Vintage, 1989)

GS *The Gay Science*, trans. Walter Kaufmann (New York, NY: Vintage, 1974)

Z *Thus Spoke Zarathustra* trans. Walter Kaufmann (New York, NY: Penguin, 1978)

Additional Texts

CD Freud, Sigmund, *Civilization and Its Discontents*, trans. James Strachey (New York, NY: W.W. Norton, 1962)

MM Beauchard, Jean-Luc, *The Mask of Memnon: Meaning and the Novel* (Eugene, OR: Cascade Books, 2022)

1 First Meeting, 01/27/2022

Mourning and Melancholia: From Trauma to *The Birth of Tragedy*

I will not begin, as is customary in small learning groups such as this, to have you go around and introduce yourselves. What does it mean to introduce oneself, anyway? In what sense is the self that I present to you the self I understand myself to be? And what is the relation between *that* self and the self underneath that self, the self that resists me, that is me and is not me, that undermines me at every turn? No, I will not ask you to introduce yourselves but will insist, rather, that you allow yourselves to be introduced to yourselves by your confrontation with the work at hand. Confrontation is the right word. For, that's just what Nietzsche's philosophy does. It confronts us, provokes us, demands of us that we push back against it and find what emerges from the struggle when either we or it has been overcome. Goading us with distorted images of ourselves, Nietzsche tells us that we are not as we think ourselves to be. Nor are we that which we discover when we peel back the layers of appearance and examine what's beneath. That too is appearance, a mask behind a mask, and the deeper we go, the more we realize that what stands behind the self is a tragic charade, the vicious circle of selves playing at selves, pantomiming around in a ring. Better then to begin with the challenge, to take Nietzsche seriously and ourselves lightly. There will be time for introductions. We will need to continuously introduce ourselves. But tonight, we must start by admitting the first principle that grounds both philosophy and psychology: We are still unable to know ourselves (*Phaedrus*, 230a). It is only by stipulating this that we can prepare ourselves for the task that lies ahead.

❖

Lacan opens *Seminar I* with the claim that in *The Interpretation of Dreams*, Freud reintroduces an essential yet neglected aspect of psychology: *meaning*. In doing so, Freud returns psychology to its philosophical roots. For, as Camus says, philosophy is at bottom about nothing but meaning—the question of meaning; the questionability of meaning; how to interpret whether our lives have a meaning, and if so, where it comes from; what such a meaning might mean to me; and so on. Philosophy, rightly understood, is the study of how

DOI: 10.4324/9781003348795-1

we construct and interpret the meaning of human life. It is, as Nietzsche will go on to say, the ordering and ranking of values, and more importantly, the arbiter of value. I want to preface our first conversation with this reflection because when I was reading through the "Attempt at Self-Criticism" with which Nietzsche opens *The Birth of Tragedy*—he wrote it fifteen years after he first wrote *Birth*, the same year he was working on *Beyond Good and Evil*—I was reminded of Lacan's appraisal of Freud, and how he saw at the foundation of the psychoanalytic method the very cornerstone Nietzsche sees as the basis of philosophical inquiry: man's search for meaning.

Turning to Nietzsche's preface, we find that the title alone gestures at this very problem. We are forced to ask what it means to proffer "An Attempt at Self-Criticism," what it means in the abstract, and more importantly, what it means *for me*. The first thing we notice is that this attempt is merely *an* attempt. Nietzsche begins by telling us that it is one of many self-criticisms, one of many attempts to understand himself. (The good critic criticizes not to denigrate but to know; the criticism of a good critic is the highest form of praise). What is more, as *Birth* will go on to demonstrate, such an attempt is destined to fail. It cannot succeed, because as Nietzsche's reflections on the Dionysian substratum of our existence reveal, there is no stable self to be criticized. There is no permanent "I" or ego that persists over time. Rather, there is in each of us a being that exists in the tension between two antagonistic drives or forces which Nietzsche calls the Apollonian and the Dionysian; indeed, we are probably nothing but the tension between these forces. (We will of course discuss Nietzsche's use of these terms in more detail later, but for now, as a little shorthand in trying to interpret and understand what Nietzsche means by the Apollonian and the Dionysian, you might think of the Apollonian as similar to Freud's Eros and the Dionysian as similar to the death drive. It's not a perfect analogy—the terms don't map onto each other one-to-one—but I found this helpful when I first read Nietzsche, having been familiar with Freud already.)

So why is it that Nietzsche begins with this attempt at self-criticism, doomed as it is to fail? Why claim to criticize a self he goes on to tell us does not exist? Moreover, if philosophy—founded as it is upon the old Delphic maxim *know thyself*—is really about understanding ourselves and constructing and interpreting the meaning of our lives, what then is behind *The Birth of Tragedy* and its search for meaning? If there is no self, as Nietzsche proposes, what are we trying to do when we seek to know ourselves? The problem at the heart of *Birth*, the problem that Nietzsche's self-criticism makes manifest, is the problem of the self, whence it arises, and how it comes to value what it values in the midst of a world of artifice and illusion. And it is in Greek tragedy, Nietzsche believes, that we find the first semblance of an answer.

❖

In the third section of *Birth*, Nietzsche recounts a story from a lost work of Aristotle's which comes to us by way of Plutarch. The story revolves around the demigod Silenus, stepfather of Dionysius, god of wine and revelry. (Silenus, you will remember, was charged with raising Dionysius. When Dionysius grew up, however, Silenus became his disciple. So, there's something fascinating in this relationship, something almost anti-Oedipal, between Silenus and Dionysius. The demigod raises the god and then becomes his devotee. And of course, in addition to intoxication and revelry, Dionysius is also the god of pain and suffering. There are stories of him being torn limb from limb, and if you've read *The Bacchae*, you know that a big part of the Dionysian cult is this idea of the world rending itself—being torn apart. So we immediately find ourselves thrown into a myth of agony and ecstasy, reversals, and the mixing up of the social order.)

In any event, in Aristotle's telling, King Mitis—the same Mitis who turned everything he touched into gold—goes hunting for Silenus with the hopes of capturing him and asking him a question. Knowing that Silenus is perpetually drunk, he expects to hear the truth in reply. (Truth can be found in wine and children, as the ancient proverb says.) Catching the demigod, Mitis asks to be told the secret of human existence. What is the meaning of life? How ought human beings to live? Now listen to Silenus' reply: "Oh wretched ephemeral race, children of chance and misery, why do you compel me to tell you what it would be most expedient for you not to hear. What is best of all is utterly beyond your reach: not to be born, not to be, to be nothing. But the second best for you is to die soon" (BT, §3). This is the rather bleak wisdom of Silenus, a wisdom which reverberates not only throughout Greek tragedy (see, for instance, Sophocles, *Oedipus at Colonus*, line 1225), but can be found even in the Gospels (see, Matthew 26:24). Life, it asserts, is nothing but pain—senseless suffering and meaningless toil—and it would be better for human beings not to exist than to have to carry the cross of existence up the hill of life, only to be nailed to it in the end.

Here, Nietzsche believes, resides the power of Greek tragedy. In this art form, more than any other, human beings are made to confront the terror of existence by looking it squarely in the face and refusing to look away. What Silenus captures with his wisdom is the traumatic knowledge that we all possess but rarely recognize—the knowledge that our lives are fleeting and destined to amount to nothing. We know we will die. We know the things we invest ourselves in will come to naught. Everything we love will go away. This is the horrifying reality that confronts us from the time of our earliest youth. (As Heidegger observes, as soon as we are born, we are old enough to die—and before that too.) But this is a horrible realization, and as soon as we recognize it, we begin finding ways to avoid it. Our lives are spent distracting ourselves from the terrible wisdom of Silenus, not thinking about it and instead focusing on unrealities that mask our vision. Yet one art form resists the temptation to veil. One finds a way to entice and charm us back to life even while presenting life in all its meanness. One depicts the absurd brutality of existence in all its terror and yet finds in that brutality, in the heart of the pain, the very reason to exist.

I'll tell you something that might surprise you, but you have to promise not to tell anyone. I'm trusting you to keep my secret, so please don't let it get out. When I drive in to campus—I live about 45 minutes away—I love to listen to trashy pop music. Whatever is on the radio, the newer, the lighter, the more ephemeral the better. I turn my speakers way up and blast it. I can't get enough. When you listen to a lot of the cheapest of cheap pop entertainment, you realize that what's most enjoyable about it is its repetitive nature. For the most part, it's all the same. It plays on the same tropes and promises the same illusions. Turn on a pop station tomorrow morning when you're driving to your office and I guarantee it won't take more than 10 minutes for you to hear a song that offers one of the following lines: "I'm going to live forever," "I'm never going to die," "I'm going to be young forever." These are the refrains repeated again and again like mantras into the ears of a very scared public. And of course, we should be scared. Because deep down we know that none of it is true. We are all going to age and deteriorate and die and, in the grand scheme of things, very soon. The songs that I listen to attempt to veil the fact that life is going away and it's going away quickly. But, as *Ecclesiastes* reminds us, "One generation departs and another generation comes ... There is no remembrance of past generations; nor will future generations be re-membered by those who come after them" (1:4–11). The reality of our sit-uation is pretty bleak.

Now, Nietzsche takes the wisdom of Silenus and doubles the terror. He not only reminds us that our lives are fleeting, that all of us are dying "With a little patience" (to quote Eliot's *The Waste Land*), but, worse still, that we are born of chance and chance governs our lives. There's a passage in *The Consolation of Philosophy* by Boethius, a medieval philosopher, in which he notes how rarely we reflect upon this preponderance of chance in our lives and how easily our lives can come to an end. He reminds us that one can wake up healthy in the morning, be bitten by a fly, and be dead by nightfall. That is human life. Here in Massachusetts, a few years back, there was this mosquito-carried disease going around called "triple e," and people were just getting bitten and dropping. But I'm bitten by mosquitos all the time. I can't live in fear of mosquitos. So I convince myself that it's just too stupid of a way to go for it to happen to me. I neglect the fact that there's no reason it shouldn't happen to me. I find ways to distract myself, to repress my fears, and to pretend I'll be fine. I have to pretend I'll be fine. We do the same thing when we exert power over others in order to make ourselves feel strong. Doing so allows us to pretend we can control our destinies. As Becker notes in *The Denial of Death*, we compensate for the fact that we lack the immortality of God by killing like God.

For Nietzsche, what's interesting about Greek tragedy is that it reveals that the Greeks did not turn away from human frailty but faced it head on. More. They deified it by putting it on stage. (The theater was to the Greek what the altar is to the Christian—the place where the divine descends into our world.) Scholars often misread Nietzsche when they assume he is prescribing a certain way of life rather than merely describing it—Nietzsche is one of the keenest observers ever to live, but rarely does he offer advice. However, here I believe is one of those rare cases where he actually gives a prescription. He thinks that if we turn toward tragedy and what the Greeks accomplished therein, we might see a life worth living for ourselves. Because what the Greeks achieve in tragedy is the ability to take the trauma of the realization of the wisdom of Silenus, of our own finite, mortal nature, our impotency, our inability to control the outcomes of our lives, and turn it into something beautiful—a work of art that makes life worth living.

The Greeks see the wisdom of Silenus, look at it honestly, and yet, do not succumb. Their pessimism does not lead to nihilism. It doesn't lead to suicide. What it does, Nietzsche thinks, is provoke a desire for *more* life—a desire to go on living. Nietzsche begins his "Attempt at Self-Criticism" with a series of provocative questions, one of which is whether there are certain pessimisms of strength. He asks, is there such a thing as a madness or neurosis of good health? What he has in mind is exactly what he thinks the Greeks achieve: an honest assessment of the bleakness of human life that gives rise to joy, excess, and an exuberance of life. But how is this possible? How could the wisdom of Silenus—the idea that it is better not to be—give rise to its opposite? How does Greek pessimism undergird Greek cheerfulness?

❖

Nietzsche tells us that in *Birth,* he sought to revolutionize how human beings interpret life. We live in a scientific age in which every phenomenon is weighed, counted, measured, and understood in terms of its facticity or truth value. But, as Socrates suggests, everything in this world has two handles, and life can also be viewed as an aesthetic phenomenon, it can be judged as a work of art. For Nietzsche, what the Greeks accomplish in tragedy is a perspective that views life not in terms of goodness and truth (i.e. morality and reason), but artfulness and beauty (i.e. invention and aesthetics). One of the great contributions of this work is Nietzsche's insistence that, when it comes to interpreting life, fiction means more than fact, lies move us more than truth, and artifice outwits nature. Nietzsche is often criticized for this—unfairly, if you ask me; for, in touting lies, he is actually being a good deal more honest than the rest of us. At the beginning of *Beyond Good and Evil*, for instance, he wonders why we are so obsessed with truth. *Why not lies? Might lies be better?* Playing the role of provocateur which suits him so well, he forces us to ask: How much of human existence—*our* existence—is constructed by us in order to help us go on living?

A few quick examples I use with my students will illustrate the point. First, consider money. Money is a very useful lie we all pretend has real value. It is a symbol, a fiction, a useless scrap of paper, or a piece of metal with no inherent use. We simply invest it with value because it helps us negotiate a myriad of relationships that require negotiating. But the truth is, if I were to leave you in the middle of the desert with a briefcase containing a million dollars, it wouldn't do you much good. Or consider my role as a professor. Why do students listen to me? They can read the texts and interpret them for themselves. My interpretations are not better simply because I have a PhD or because I've been hired to teach. Why do you listen to me? What gives me the authority to tell you what this book says or means? You simply go along with the charade because the lie of authority tricks you into believing that there are people out there you can turn to when you are scared or in need or confused. Or, again, think about walking down the hall in a public building. In this country, we all walk on the right side of a corridor. Why do we do that? It's an unwritten rule, which of course is a fiction, a lie to which we acquiesce, that regulates our behavior and helps us to get along. We treat the lie as if it has some deep, metaphysical truth behind it—you should see how irate I get when someone is walking on the wrong side through one of the academic buildings here on campus—but, in point of fact, there is no order to existence beyond that which we impose upon it.

Measurement, time, and morality—these things are all very useful, and Nietzsche is not suggesting that we get rid of them. What he is showing us is that no matter how useful they are, they are also constructed by us, fictions to help us get through life. And so, he asks us to consider whether human life is rooted more in truth, what he calls the scientific or moral worldview, or in lies, the aesthetic worldview. For Nietzsche, the answer is obvious. The artistic view of life is actually truer than the view that there is some objective truth to which we can all conform or subscribe. Even the idea of an objective standard of truth is a fiction that depends on the construction of a perspective that does not exist. There is no objectivity. There is no independent, external reality somewhere beyond the human frame. Or, if there is some kind of God's-eye view of existence, we don't have it. We cannot access it. And so, for us, it's as if it doesn't exist at all.

Lyn: *Can I come in and ask a quick question?*

Absolutely.

Lyn: *Could you speak a bit about Nietzsche's philosophical context—what is the lineage of his thought, who are the contemporaries he is addressing or arguing against?*

Nietzsche views the history of philosophy, the history of ideas, as a conversation between the few great thinkers, and naturally, he numbers himself among them. So, who is he responding to? First, Plato. He sees himself as being in competition with—perhaps also a disciple of—Plato, who is a major conversation partner for him. More contemporary is Schopenhauer. Nietzsche is writing *Birth* in the years after doing a thorough study of Schopenhauer, and he claimed that Schopenhauer was one of the few thinkers he respected. You could say that Schopenhauer awakened Nietzsche to the pessimistic view of life, to the wisdom of Silenus. But Schopenhauer argues that we end there, that we end with the nihilism—life is not worth living. Nietzsche agrees with Schopenhauer to a point. He starts writing *Birth* at the outbreak of the Franco-Prussian War, one of the first really modern wars with modern technology and artillery being used. Before he finishes writing *Birth*, he goes to the front, where he is a medical orderly caring for the wounded and dying. He sees the savagery and barbarism of modern warfare. He gets dysentery, returns home, and for the rest of his life, has crippling physical ailments. He can barely eat without being bedridden for days with stomach problems, and he has horrible migraines. In the later years of his life, he's losing his sight, and then ultimately, I think most people know, he goes mad and spends his last decade as basically an invalid being cared for by his sister.

So, for Nietzsche, it's important to write this work, having seen what he's seen and dealt with the suffering he's dealt with, because he looks back on the influence of Schopenhauer and finds that Schopenhauer's nihilism is something of a luxury. You can be nihilistic and say life is not worth living if you go to the opera and have fancy dinners like Schopenhauer did. If your life is pretty good, then it's okay to be a nihilist. But if your life is terrible, as Nietzsche's became, if you've seen the horrors of the world, then you need a reason to go on. And that's what he's looking for, I think, in the Greeks. He's looking for examples of people who have seen the worst of life and yet have found a reason to go on. And Sophocles or Euripides or whoever—they're writing through the Peloponnesian War and plague and the oligarchy of the Thirty Tyrants who came into power in Athens and slaughtered five percent of the Athenian population. They're seeing the horrors of life in all its brutality and yet they are writing these beautiful masterpieces and giving people a reason to live. That's really what Nietzsche wants to understand. He wants a reason to live that he thinks is hard-won because it has dealt with the reality of existence.

Orna: *Could you elaborate on the aesthetic view of life and how it is connected to lies?*

In my reading, Nietzsche is picking up a line of thinking that is present in the works of Plato. Scholars don't usually emphasize it, but Plato has this idea that we need to be charmed into continued existence, that there needs to be something that entices us to go on living. For Nietzsche, the thing that does this is art. He says that life without art is unlivable. Art takes trauma and doesn't stay with the traumatic moment but sublimates it into something else: tragedy. Of course, tragedy is still painful. It represents or depicts suffering. But it does so in such a way that we can live through it by making it part of a story, by making it someone else's suffering. We can see ourselves in someone else's suffering in a work of art. For example, I've written some fiction, and I always realize after the fact that what I've done is taken something that was traumatic for me and turned it into a story. But I'm not thinking about it when I create characters and build their world. I'm just telling a story about people who seem completely unrelated to me. For Nietzsche, what art, and tragedy in particular, can do is provide a way to move through trauma toward something else. It's a way of not ignoring it or pretending it didn't happen, but taking the traumatic moment and turning it into something that makes life worth living for us and for other people. We can see our lives in a work of fiction, see the beauty in it, and want to go on living because of that.

James: *There's a clear analogy in psychoanalysis of delving into trauma and developing a capacity to create something in the place of what has been destroyed by the trauma.*

Yes, I think psychoanalysis is very much concerned with doing the same type of work—getting me to be able to take my traumas and turn them into the story of my life or see how they fit into the story of my life. Of course, for Nietzsche, the story of my life is a fiction. I create a work of art and call it "the story of my life" which I fit this traumatic moment into. When Nietzsche talks about the Apollonian impulse (this is one artistic drive—the Dionysian is a different one, and in *Birth* he sees them working in tandem), he says the best analogy we can give is dreams. Dreams are Apollonian constructs. In relation to our dreams, Nietzsche claims, we are all artists. We are creating worlds in our dream states. This is not so different from Freud. The dreams of war trauma he describes in *Beyond the Pleasure Principle*, in which the dream that recurs is not really a dream but a return to the traumatic moment, actually represents the inability to dream. It is not being able to have a full dream in which everything seems to make sense (at least so long as one is sleeping) that underscores the trauma. The goal of the analyst is to get the analysand to return to the creative state of constructing dreams. The goal is to turn the analysand into an artist, someone who can dream in such a way that he's making a work of art in his dreams.

Jason: *I think the key word there is* sublimation, *which of course is key for psychoanalysis. I think sublimation is that transformation of something drive-based or trauma-based into something higher that Nietzsche would call art, or that Freud would call functioning in the world.*

Absolutely. For Nietzsche, what the Greeks do exceptionally well is sublimate the trauma of existence into beautiful works of art. We still read Greek tragedies. Of course, he mentions Shakespeare in *Birth* as well. Every great work of art is doing this in some sense—taking the trauma, sublimating it into something, creating something else out of it, and making life worth living. That is the heart of what he's after in this text.

❖

As we said, Nietzsche thinks that at bottom there is no self, but merely the tension between the Apollonian and Dionysian. Now, all the lies we were mentioning—morality, rules, laws, the different fictions of social life— are sublimations in some sense. They are all human creations beyond just the brute trauma of existence. But Nietzsche thinks there are better and worse ways of sublimating. For him, there are two elements to human existence. The Dionysian, we have said, is the traumatic truth of our finitude, our frailty, our dependence, our inability to control our circumstances, and of course, our mortality. The Dionysian realization lends itself to a certain type of sublimation, a certain type of art. It's characterized by intoxication and ecstasy. Think of when you go to a concert and lose yourself in the music. You're completely swept up in it and everything else fades away. There's a sense of intoxication and revelry. Nietzsche gives an example of these festivals that were held throughout Europe from ancient times through the Middle Ages, like the Feast of Fools, where a prisoner would become king for a day. Or peasants would become bishops of the church and everyone would get drunk and act foolishly. The low would replace the high and the whole structure and ordering of the world would be revealed for what it is—mere construction. But the best example of Dionysian sublimation for Nietzsche is music, in particular a certain type of music that captivates people and causes them to lose themselves in it.

Apollonian sublimation, on the other hand, leads to the artifice we mentioned earlier—the ordering and structuring of society, moral rules and regulations, a will to truth, and a desire for (certain kinds of) knowledge. In the art world, it is characterized by symmetry and geometry. It is sculpture and architecture, the most concrete and least abstract forms of art. The Apollonian and the Dionysian, Nietzsche says, are always warring against one another. There's an antagonism at the heart of things. This plays out on the social level—think of the two impulses always in conflict in politics: authoritarianism, the highly regimented social order, and anarchy, freedom from all external restraints—as well as at the level of the individual. An example I use with my students is something I do all the time: At the beginning of a new semester, I have plans for what I want to accomplish and I set up a very regimented schedule. I'm going to get up every morning at 5, go for a run, walk the dog, check my emails, write, do this, do that. It's a very Apollonian structure I've made for myself. Life becomes very orderly and rigid—for about a week. And during that time, I'm hugely productive. Then one night, for no reason at all, I stay up until 2 in the morning drinking and watching reruns of *Seinfeld* on TV. And when that alarm goes off, because the structure is still in place, I'm miserable and I wonder why I did this to myself. And of course, the answer is that my Dionysian impulse for excess, for freedom from the structure, for chaos, bursts through the Apollonian regimen I had set up. It must do so. And then, because the Dionysian gets in the way of my productivity and functioning in the world, I need to put the Apollonian structure back in place. I come down hard with an even stricter regime.

These two drives are always antagonizing one another and breaking through one another in order to express themselves in our lives. What Nietzsche wants to know is if there's a way for them to "incite each other to new and more powerful births" (BT, §1). That is, is it possible to play the Apollonian and the Dionysian off of one another in such a way as to synthesize them rather than letting each continually suppress and undermine the other? This is what he thinks is accomplished in Greek tragedy. It is an art form that is both Apollonian and Dionysian: Apollonian in that you have the individual stories of individual characters who have real problems, moral quandaries, and questions that demand factual answers. Oedipus is a great example. Initially, Oedipus' whole life can be thought of in Apollonian terms. He is an individual trying to make his way through existence, trying to interpret life, finding meaning in certain things, solving the mystery of the Sphinx. And then the Dionysian element comes in and upends everything. Suddenly, he's awakened to the fact that he didn't know what was going on in his life, he was deluded all along. The meaning he had constructed was false and now he has to live through the trauma after the fact and find a way to go on. In the end, he does find a way to go on. Blinded and crippled with age, a patricide who unknowingly married his mother, Oedipus concludes that "all is well."

Camus calls this declaration sacred. I think Nietzsche would agree. For, if *Birth* suggests anything, it's that we ought to live as if we are characters on the Greek stage. We are all Oedipuses, blindly making our way through a traumatic world and having to go on living in spite of the pain all around us, the pain we harbor within us. The tragedies don't usually end with the death of the protagonist (though sometimes they do). Often the protagonist has to make his way through life after the traumatic event. Nietzsche is offering an interpretation of life as a work of art, one in which we see ourselves as characters in the divine comedy, as he calls it. Of course, he is referencing Dante, but he isn't worried about whether or not there is a spectator watching the show. It is enough to know that we are on stage, the curtain is up, and we have the ability to play our parts. It is left to us to play them. The question is, are we up for the performance?

❖

Suzanne: *I feel like someone should write a book on parenting based on this, because parenting is like living through a tragedy in a way. It's like you thought you knew everything, and you actually knew nothing. And then you're watching these other tragedies unfolding in front of you, and you can't really intervene, like to write the story for them. They have to live it.*

Absolutely. I have three kids and something I've realized in parenting is that I'm constantly confronted with my own impotency. I can't protect these people whom I'm tasked with protecting. It's Oedipal, really. As a parent, you have this responsibility, you are in this situation and have to figure it out. And at the same time, you are aware that you have no idea how to do anything and that at any moment things could go horribly wrong and the whole structure could collapse. And so, you're caught in this tension: on the one hand, the utter responsibility, and on the other hand, your utter inability to live up to it. It is very much the tragic situation. Now the question is, how do you live in the face of that? How do you live through it?

Suzanne: *You go back to school after thirty years, that's what I did. Because there's also this sense of a loss of meaning. Your children grow up and they can't be your whole meaning anymore. But you have to keep on living.*

Right. The question for Nietzsche is always just that. When we're confronted with this loss of meaning, which of course, the rupture of the chaos of the Dionysian does for us, we realize that the meaning we had constructed was illusory and now it's gone. What do we do with that? Where do we go from there? It's an attempt to reconstruct meaning with the knowledge underneath it—the understanding that it too will be toppled in time. It too will be destroyed. For Nietzsche, it's this constant process of creating something that gives us the ability to live and helps us make sense out of life, but always knowing that that thing too will be destroyed, and we will have to do it all over again. We'll deal with other ruptures, other traumas, and then we'll have to do it again. He always wants to challenge us to be enticed back to life—to keep coming back to the proverbial well. He says of the Greeks that they reverse the wisdom of Silenus to such a degree that to die becomes for them worst of all and second worst is to die soon. To use your example of parenting, I used to think before I was a parent, when I had no real responsibility for anyone but myself, that everyone dies and it's no big deal. Now, death is a crushing reality for me. I cannot die. Not just because I have a responsibility to my kids and my family, but because they have enticed me back to life, just as Nietzsche wants for us.

Jason: *I have a comment and a question. First, I disagree with your Eros/Thanatos division. For me, Freud sees the ego and the id as complementary. He describes them as being like a rider and a horse. Without the horse, the rider*

> *cannot get anywhere, and without the rider, the horse is wild and aimless. One tames and structures the other, and together they can go far. My question is, in terms of the Apollonian being individualistic and the Dionysian being collectivistic, how would you say that fits into things?*

First, in *The Ego and the Id*, Freud says that the way the two relate in the horse/rider analogy is that the rider, or the ego, thinks he is leading the horse, whereas really the horse, the id, takes them where it wants to go. The rider is sort of lying to himself. In this sense, it is a really nice pairing with the Apollonian and the Dionysian.

Jason: So, are we unable to save our world? If there's no saving us, how do we go on living?

There's only enticement back to life. And to your question about how individuality relates to the Apollonian and Dionysian, what Nietzsche says is that individuality—thinking of yourself as an individual—is an Apollonian illusion. And of course, this is coming from Schopenhauer. This is why I said in the beginning that there is no self, at bottom, for Nietzsche. At bottom is the Dionysian truth that we will fade into nothingness. Artistically, the Dionysian is fusion into unity. Think about when you're drunk. You like being drunk not because you feel more like yourself, but because you forget yourself. You lose yourself and are free to talk, to engage, and to say things you wouldn't normally say. Your eye ceases to be turned in on yourself and you forget, momentarily, your own self-consciousness. The Dionysian is a kind of loss into oblivion, a spreading out of the self into what Nietzsche calls the "primal unity of the world." At bottom, we are all connected in that we all suffer. There's a community of suffering, a collective of pain. The Apollonian, on the other hand, gives rise to the self because of all the ways we understand and interpret ourselves through rules, laws, morality, and identifying character traits—all of the ways I might tell you who I am. These are delimiting constructs, which are Apollonian in nature.

Jason: Back to Lacan, this thing called "Matthew" or "Jason," that's a construct.

Yes, that's what individuality is. For Nietzsche, beneath that self is just chaos. To bring things back to psychoanalytic thought, when you have a newborn child, you really realize this. A newborn is just a chaotic bundle of drives and desires. All of the ordering comes from Apollonian constructions.

Mary: This is my first-time reading Nietzsche, and I was struck by how beautiful the writing is. I was wondering about his understanding of beauty—is it transcendence, is it escape?

I love reading Nietzsche. I was an English major in college and I really appreciate good writing. Most philosophers are horrendous writers. But Nietzsche, Camus, and even Freud are a pleasure to read because they care about style. And I think Nietzsche is trying in his philosophy to approximate what he sees in the art he admires. It's right to observe how he writes and to notice that it's beautiful. I think he believes that philosophy at its best can do what art does and maybe even do it better. To your question, he wouldn't deny that art is an escape from the trauma of existence, but, importantly, it's not an escape that denies the reality of the trauma. Rather, it situates it. It finds a place for it.

Nietzsche is a perspectivist, meaning that he doesn't believe in an objective truth. There are only various perspectives: scientific, aesthetic, religious, and so forth. But just because there isn't an objective truth doesn't mean that there can't be better and worse perspectives. Some perspectives tell us more about existence. They encompass more, contain more, make more sense out of life, and are better for us. They make us want to live more. For Nietzsche, certain escapisms, such as the religious one, are worse because they try to ignore suffering or offer as an answer to it something beyond this life. They don't keep us wanting to be engaged with life and wanting to go on living. So, yes, I think he would say art is a type of escape, but it's a better and broader one, and preferable to pretty much anything else, from his perspective.

James: *I'm thinking about that space between mourning and melancholia, how it's filled with tension. But so often we avoid the grief to avoid admitting whatever has been lost. There's a tendency for patients to skip the mourning and go straight to melancholia.*

For Freud and Nietzsche, who are both pessimistic—or rather tragic—thinkers, we are constantly living in this state of tension. That's what life is, essentially, for both of them: tension. And the question is, what do we do about it? How do we live? In *Civilization and Its Discontents*, for all his critiques of civilization, Freud is very much on the side of civilization. He thinks it's preferable, for all its faults, to the alternatives. And I think that's how Nietzsche thinks about art and tragedy. We're born into a horrible situation. What's the best we can do? We can accomplish some pretty remarkable things with art. We can turn the horrors of existence into something beautiful. And in experiencing that beauty, we want to go on living and say "yes" to life. For Nietzsche, the most life-affirming thing you can do is say "yes" to your life as it is and not want anything about it to be different. Could I love my life enough—could I be happy enough with my life, joyful enough about my life—that I wouldn't want to change anything that's ever happened? And he thinks we're capable of doing that if we can tell really great stories about ourselves, if we can create really great narratives of what it means to be the beings that we are. He wants us to be great artists of our own lives.

Orna: This creation of narratives for our lives seems to imply crafting stories that may not really represent our constructed, that is, Apollonian, realities. And that would seem to take a superior view of the Dionysian, instead of holding it on equal footing in a give-and-take with the Apollonian. Is that a fair assessment?

That's a great observation, Orna. Kaufmann, the translator and editor of the edition we're reading, writes in a footnote that Nietzsche in later works gives up on the Apollonian and is only concerned with the Dionysian. I don't think that's right. He might not mention the Apollonian explicitly, but for me, tracking through Nietzsche's works, it's always the two in conjunction with one another that gives us the ability to go on. The Dionysian may get at the truth of things, but we need lies. We cannot function without lies. The constructive aspect of the Apollonian art can't be done to the exclusion of the Dionysian, or *vice versa*. And when in conjunction with one another, they have a synergistic effect.

Lyn: Does the Dionysian also bring into the fold a greater sense of beauty and spontaneity?

Yes, absolutely. The Dionysian is on the one hand the terror and chaos and suffering of existence. But on the other hand, it is the spontaneity, joy, excess—being overfull with vivacity, overflowing with life. I mean, the word "birth" in the title is important because it calls forth an image of the art being created here as being birthed from an excess. But birth is also agony. It is also torment and sometimes death. The Apollonian—the rigid structure—needs the excess, exuberance, and ecstasy that the Dionysian provides—that brings it back to life—but it also attempts to tame the beast, so to speak, and provide some sedatives to help with the Dionysian pain.

A.M. Pelos: It's like, you need an editor at some point. I mean, you can write until you're blue in the face, but sooner or later you've got to come in and do some shaping.

Jean-Luc: On the other hand, if you don't lose yourself in the writing, it won't be very interesting. You have to have that freedom too, or else your writing will end up—

A.M. Pelos: … putting everyone to sleep.

Jean-Luc: That's right.

2 Second Meeting, 02/24/2022
The Value of Values: The Psychology of Morals

I want to begin our discussion of Nietzsche's *On the Genealogy of Morals* by drawing our attention to its subtitle, "A Polemic," and asking: a polemic against what? There are, of course, answers that come readily to mind: slave or herd morality, the politics of *ressentiment*, modern democratic ideals, the kind of social and political leveling which, in its demand for equality, demeans that which is exceptional, etc. Each of these is, in a sense, a correct answer to the question raised above. And each, in another sense, is incorrect. That is to say that the standard readings of *Genealogy* both help to illuminate the text and to make it more opaque. Many readers of Nietzsche would argue that *Genealogy* is his clearest, most straightforward work, a text in which he lays out in fairly precise terms his arguments against the leveling taking place in modern European society. (This is why it is the book most likely to be taught to undergraduates.) He sees this leveling as an effort to make human beings tamer, safer, more mediocre, more equal (and thus less true to life), more sterile, less dangerous, but also less awe-inspiring, less real, more removed from the essence of what we really are. I won't discount these readings. They're valuable and, to an extent, accurate. But in my opinion, they neglect and even obscure one of Nietzsche's most profound insights.

Nietzsche begins his preface by telling us that "we are unknown to ourselves, we men of knowledge," we are strangers to ourselves, and each of us is "furthest from himself" (GM, "Preface," §1). What he means, I think, is that we are always looking for answers outside of ourselves, searching for knowledge and meaning in the external world rather than within. This is a fundamentally human problem: To be self-conscious means existing at a distance from oneself, living at a remove from one's own experience. As human beings, we are creatures who are not what we are. Unlike my dog, who is completely what he is and cannot be otherwise, who is fully present to himself and his experiences and never reflects back upon them, I stand at a distance from myself and see myself as something to be examined, questioned, understood. My conception of myself is bound up with memories and projections—that is, thoughts of the past and future. I remember the Matthew I used to be, the one who fits into the narrative I tell myself about my life, and

DOI: 10.4324/9781003348795-2

I fantasize about the Matthew I will be, thus projecting that narrative forward. But I never quite know who I am in the present, never experience my experiences without already standing outside of them and reflecting upon them.

In drawing this out, Nietzsche is tapping into the idea that humans are fundamentally temporal beings and that our consciousness is characterized by time. And this, in turn, helps to explain one of his more significant insights in this text: Human beings are value-making creatures. The fact that we are always at a remove from ourselves, that we do not define ourselves as what we are, but what we want to be and what we seek, means that our own self-understanding is dictated by what we value. My conception of myself is rooted not in what I experience but what I value most. This, I think, is the central point of the first essay of *Genealogy*. What Nietzsche wants to get us to ask is: What is it that we value, why do we value what we value, what is the value of that which we value, and ultimately, how do these things shape the way we understand and interpret ourselves? Or as he puts it at the end of the first essay, "All the sciences have from now on to prepare the way for the future task of the philosophers: this task understood as the solution of the *problem of value*, the determination of the *order of rank among values*" (GM, I, §17).

What Nietzsche is advocating is a kind of psychological turn. He wants us to stop seeking knowledge *out there*, in the world, and start seeking to understand what is at bottom in us, what drives us to do the things we do, and make the choices that we make. For him, the modus operandi of human life is that which one values most. Whatever we care for is going to be that which propels us forward both as individuals and also collectively as a species. Nietzsche quotes approvingly from the Gospel of Matthew, "Where your treasure is, there will your heart be also." That is, human behavior can only be understood if one understands what it aims at. What idols do we worship? What ideals have we set as our ultimate good?

When I teach *Genealogy* to my undergrads, I usually pause at this point, pick a student at random, and ask him his major. At Boston College, chances are he answers economics or finance or something like that. And so, I'll press him: Why are you majoring in economics? And he'll say it's because he wants to manage hedge funds. Again, I'll ask him why. And he'll say, "Well, I want to earn a good salary and have benefits and stability." I'll continue to press him: Why? And he'll say something about wanting to support a family and own a house and maybe go on nice vacations. Again, why? And he'll think a bit and come up with something like, "Well, that's what my parents did, but I'm not really sure." And ultimately, if I keep pushing the question why, the student ends up admitting that what he wants is to be happy, and he believes that these things will make him happy. This is not a new point that Nietzsche is making here, but part of what he is articulating is that we do the things we do because we think they are good for us and will lead to our happiness in the end. That's what motivates our choices—big choices and small choices alike. There is always something driving our decisions and it is always what we think is best for us. Why do I go to the gym instead of reading a book? Because I value health over intelligence. Why do I stay up late drinking whiskey rather than getting to bed early? Because I value pleasure over health. There is always some value orienting my choices, even if I haven't fully articulated it to myself or understood it myself.

Nietzsche tells us that human beings are the types of creatures that cannot *not* pursue some value. We cannot not be working toward some aim, purpose, or goal. He ends *Genealogy* by concluding that "man would rather will *nothingness* than *not* will" (GM, III, §28). That is, we are incapable of acting without an end in mind. We need to have a goal, to be striving toward something. And we will find even bad reasons to do a thing rather than have no reason at all. Think of all the miserable, tedious jobs people hate doing and don't want to do. Still, we find a way to do them by telling ourselves that what we want to accomplish is something else and that this job we hate is in service of that thing we want. So, we are valuing something that is a level removed from what we're doing, but we're always valuing *something*. What Nietzsche wants is for us to try to decipher what that something is. And, as it turns out, a lot of our values are only implicitly held. We assume them without identifying them or considering whether they are actually good for us or worth valuing.

What orients our values most, Nietzsche says, is the system of morality to which we adhere. (Perhaps values and morality are inseparable from one another in that every value suggests a means of pursuing it, an *ought* to follow upon an established *is*. Freud seems to suggest this, insisting that there is no more deeply held or psychologically significant value than an explicitly moral one.) Morality is the cornerstone of civilization, the instrument we use to train our children, to socialize them, and to teach them how to live with one another. And as we have said, the highest of all moral values is the idea of the good. For us, living in a post-Christian society—Nietzsche is writing after Darwin, as the final bell tolls on Christendom—the idea of the good is bound up with notions of selflessness, humility, modesty, a desire for truth. But is it obvious, Nietzsche wants us to ask, that selflessness is a valuable thing? What happens when we question the values we assume unreflectively from the society in which we live?

Nietzsche begins by objecting to those who assume the utility of a value like selflessness and then deem it good based on the circular logic of its supposed use. He wants to investigate how we come to hold the values we do and why we see them as essential aspects of the good life. Is a life based on such moral valuations actually good? In what sense? And what is being diminished or demeaned by pursuing an existence such as the one that these values prescribe? To answer these questions, we must look to the origin of such values. Of course, any idea of the good around which people orient their behavior is good for someone. But *cui bono?* as Cicero was wont to ask. Selflessness, humility, equality, pity—each of these moral ideals benefits some and harms others.

The question one must ask is: who stands to gain and at what price? And, of paramount concern to Nietzsche, is the question of whether such commitments further human life or threaten to reduce it.

This is the point at which an alternate reading of the text emerges. Nietzsche teases out the dichotomies of noble versus ascetic values and aristocratic society versus slave morality. But there is more to the idea of slave morality that he develops. It is certainly true that Nietzsche believes the ascetic morality of self-abnegation arises out of resentment—the resentment of the weak for their betters—and that such slave morality, born of Judeo-Christian ideals such as pity for the oppressed and damnation for the strong, is a tool used by inferiors to hold down their betters. And it is true that he sees in such efforts a degeneration of the human animal—something unnatural and nihilistic, something that reveals a sense of nausea, a profound discontent with life. But in §11 of the first essay, we find reason to suspect that this polemic is not aimed at a certain type of morality—say, the priestly morality, as opposed to the noble, aristocratic morality—but morality itself. Morality, he suggests, cannot but be used as a tool for the reduction and destruction of human beings. Remember that this work is called *On the Genealogy of Morals*. Note that it does not specify *which* morals. It is about the genealogy of morality itself:

> Supposing that what is at any rate believed to be the "truth" really is true, and the *meaning of all culture* is the reduction of the beast of prey "man" to a tame and civilized animal, a *domestic animal*, then one would undoubtedly have to regard all those instincts of reaction and *ressentiment* through whose aid the noble races and their ideals were finally confounded and overthrown as the actual *instruments of culture* (GM, I, §11).

Here we have Nietzsche saying that it is not slave morality *per se* that is the reduction of the noble ideal, but culture itself, civilization itself, every moral valuation. He suggests that we are all members of the priestly caste, all motivated by the politics of resentment, all guilty of harboring nihilistic ill-will toward life. And he, most of all, is like the ascetic priest: cunning, malicious, resentful, deceptive, weak. Nietzsche is describing himself as a philosopher, using intellect as a tool against those who are physically stronger. He diagnoses slave morality and the mentality of slave morality so well because he understands it in himself.

To bring things back to where we started, recall that *Genealogy* is a polemic against us—we "men of knowledge" who don't know ourselves and, more importantly, don't want to know ourselves. Fueled by resentment, we seek knowledge outside ourselves and identify evil "out there" because we cannot reckon with the insignificance and mediocrity we find within. The book Nietzsche writes prior to *Genealogy* is *Beyond Good and Evil*. It's worth noting that the dichotomy of good and evil, which Nietzsche links with slave morality, derives from the Adamic myth in the Book of Genesis. We gain the concepts of "good" and "evil" when we eat from the tree of knowledge. So, to have knowledge and to be a human being living in the world, living in society, is to live under the sign of good and evil. To get beyond this would be to try to find a way out of what we fundamentally are: Moral beings trapped in society using morality as a tool to keep each other in check and dictate our own behavior. Freud makes a similar point about morality being the foundation of social life. For him, civilization only exists when the weak band together to restrain the strong. Thus, to live in civilization is to take part in furthering the slave morality that Nietzsche bemoans. To hold values, to be a moral creature, and to be a human being is to be subject to the kind of asceticism that removes us from nature and leads to a poisoned and degenerate form of life. The problem is, there is no exit now.

❖

Jason: Could you unpack a bit more what Nietzsche means by "ressentiment?" What I think he's describing is envy—a hatred and jealousy, but also a desire to destroy that thing of which one is envious. I'm thinking of the passage where he says that the saints' joy is heightened when they get to see the sinners burn. And I'm wondering why he specifically uses the French word "ressentiment" instead of the word for "envy" in German.

For Nietzsche, *ressentiment* is a reactive impulse. An adherent to noble morality glories and revels in himself, finds happiness in himself, and only takes notice of his other—that is, his inferiors—incidentally. A noble soul doesn't base its view of itself on the other and doesn't envy the other. Rather, it sees the other as something to compete with, something against which to sharpen itself. *Ressentiment*, on the other hand, is fundamentally reactionary in that it first sees the greatness outside itself and hates it. And so, it bases its conception of evil on the other and regards itself—in opposition to the other—as good.

An example I like to use for the noble ideal is Michael Jordon. Jordon is a malicious competitor. He doesn't care if people don't like him and doesn't really conform to what most would think of as a "good" human being or "nice guy." Instead, he revels in dominating others (both on and off the court). Many musicians, artists, authors are hypercompetitive—they enjoy flexing their muscles and being the best at what they do. *Ressentiment* reacts to this show of strength with contempt and envy: "It's evil to be that way. Where's his humility?" Nietzsche uses the analogy of how lambs view wolves. To the lamb, it's evil to be a wolf. Why can't wolves be gentle like us? Why can't they be good little lambs? But in reality, wolves are just being what they are when they devour lambs. To ask them to be otherwise is to demand of wolves that they not be wolves. What Nietzsche sees in our moral values are systems of power set up to make it seem as though mediocrity is good and excellence and pride over excellence are bad. He suggests that we shouldn't be restraining people from feeling proud of their accomplishments. Rather, we should be encouraging them to always strive to do better.

David: Could you talk about Nietzsche's use of language around Aryans and Judaism?

In Nietzsche's writing, we find nothing but disdain for anti-Semites. He thinks that such bigotry represents a stunted and intellectually anemic worldview. Unfortunately, his sister married a notorious anti-Semite, and when he came under her care after he lost his mind in the last decade of his life, she edited many of his works and published them as first editions. As a result, Nietzsche was taken up early on by the National Socialist movement and seen as supportive of such ideas. But it couldn't be further from how Nietzsche viewed things.

When he is talking about Judaism, he is talking about a value system that takes the weak to be strong—you know, "blessed are the poor" and so on. Nietzsche's father was a Lutheran pastor, so he was reading Judaism as a precursor to Christian ideals and Christian values (what in theological terms is called *supersessionism*). He thinks Christianity inherits the core of its value system from Judaism—one that praises weakness, humility, and pity and desires to hold down strength. But Nietzsche is a very complicated thinker. In his autobiography, *Ecco Homo*, he says that he's always most critical of the things he values most. He says that he only criticizes the best thoughts and ideas and thinkers who have ever lived. So, he is criticizing the Jewish value system of selflessness, humility, care for the poor, pity for the weak and downtrodden, etc., because he sees it as reducing human beings down to the level of mediocrity and weakness. But in doing so, he is also holding it up as one of the most interesting and revolutionary achievements in human history. He tells us that it represents a reevaluation of a previous value system that paved the way for humans to become intelligent. Prior to Judeo-Christian morality, it was physical strength that conquered. The strong few preyed on the weak many. Aristocratic societies of the ancient world were run by small factions of rich, powerful warrior types who held everyone else down. Intellect wasn't the prevailing force. Nietzsche sees the development in morality introduced by Judaism as a drug in the sense of being both a poison and a cure. Cunning, intellect, development of an interiority, learning how to outwit others—these things are a boon for humanity.

The problem, Nietzsche thinks, is that a certain value system, such as the Judeo-Christian one, will get us to a certain point of development, but then cease to be beneficial. It will be valuable initially, then at a certain point will start to atrophy and slouch toward something that is no longer useful. The noble ideal runs its course to some extent, then you have the reevaluation of values with Judaism and Christianity which take us further down the road. But he thinks humanity is starting to atrophy again and slouch toward nihilism.

It's time for something new to emerge and pave the path forward. I don't think that Nietzsche wants to return us to a world wherein strength reigns supreme. That's a misreading of this text. What we need is something new to take us further than we have previously gone. And we will always have to keep reinventing ourselves when our value systems become useless in some way.

Suzanne: *In §11, Nietzsche talks about how people can hold themselves in check when they're among equals, but in the encounter with the stranger, they return to being triumphant monsters. When I was reading this, I was reminded of the January 6 insurrection, and I'm curious to hear your thoughts.*

Yes, so Nietzsche is always provocative and giving us challenging things to think about. At times he refers to historical and political figures as examples who embody his ideals—Napoleon, for instance. But more often, I think the better examples are great artists. As we saw in *The Birth of Tragedy*, Nietzsche is very concerned with art and thinks that art has a fundamental role to play in human life. In the second essay of *Genealogy*, we'll see that he talks about these "beasts of prey" as artists who are creating a new world. For him, the truly great artists will always be both: in communion with one another, appreciating, reveling in their art together, and at times seeking to destroy others who are not as good, who are less than themselves. I'm reminded of the Woody Allen movie *Midnight in Paris*. The main character gives Ernest Hemmingway his novel and asks him to read it. And immediately, Hemmingway says that he hates it and hands it back to him. He says, "Either it's good writing, in which case I'll hate it because I'll be worried that it's better than mine, or it's bad writing, in which case I hate it because I hate bad writing." It's this kind of thing that I think Nietzsche finds going on in great artists.

Of course, the artistic impulse stands behind a lot of politics as well. It's amazing how many political leaders are failed artists: Hitler, Mussolini, Churchill. It's as if they're trying to bring their artistic expressions into the world; only because they couldn't do it in the art world, they do it in the world of politics. I think Nietzsche would agree that there's a parallel between those two things. He is trying to look at the world amorally, meaning that there will be events where people do monstrous things; considered morally, they're terrible, but considered aesthetically, they might be great. That's how he sees someone like Napoleon. Morally, he is monstrous, but aesthetically, he accomplishes beautiful things.

Andrew: *I think it can be really challenging at times to sympathize with Nietzsche's perspective on this. I'm thinking, for example, of the news this morning about Putin invading Ukraine. On the other hand, I think a good real-world example of the leveling and the problems with slave morality is how social media—this sort of groupthink en masse—can be really soul-crushing to people on the receiving end of its scorn. Often those under attack are the very people who are the best in their respective fields—actors, artists, politicians. Not to say that they shouldn't be held accountable for their actions, but it's problematic when it's just about freedom of speech or freedom of thought. And I think people really love to tear down big names, delight in it even. Also, I was reading Foucault's* Discipline and Punish *recently, and I think there are a lot of parallels with* Genealogy.

Absolutely—Foucault pulls from Nietzsche extensively on the foundations of punishment. But to your first point, one thing that is important to understand when reading Nietzsche (and it is often misunderstood about him) is that he's not always prescribing what he thinks things should look like. In fact, I think he's usually resisting the temptation to do so. He describes things as he thinks they are, as he sees them. So, it can come across as if he's championing these "beasts of prey," for instance, when he is actually using provocative rhetoric and an abrasive style to provoke and challenge us. He forces us to think through these things and confront them: If this is what's going on—if we talk about justice, for instance, when we really care about power—then do we accept things as they are, or are we driven to change?

To your second point, I think you're right on this. We often see how stifling the herd mentality, as Nietzsche would call it, can be—especially for someone who doesn't want to think the way everyone else does. That person is often seen as dangerous to the collective (and he might actually be dangerous, by the way). Today's events are a great example. Someone like Putin, who doesn't want to sit with the status quo but wants to reshape the world the way he thinks it ought to be, can be very dangerous. Yet there are also examples of great artists and political figures who have had visions of a different world and were up against the herd mentality, but they broke through and did revolutionary things that, in hindsight, we would all agree furthered human existence: the founding fathers, Dr. King, Socrates, Galileo, just to name a few off the top of my head. These may be less controversial, but you could also look at someone like Alexander the Great, who is estimated to be responsible for hundreds of thousands of deaths, yet his campaigns directly led to the exchange of information, knowledge, languages, and cultures that undoubtedly advanced human civilization to a significant degree. So, Nietzsche doesn't want to live in a world where we don't have people trying to break through that group mentality.

Jason: *To me that sounds extremely Darwinian, and I wonder to what extent Nietzsche must've been influenced by Darwin. Darwin would say that humanity doesn't evolve through ordinary garden-variety* Homo sapiens, *but through those rare, spontaneous mutations that are somehow exceptional. Sometimes they're disasters. But we need these exceptions to move forward as a species.*

Yes, Nietzsche is writing not long after Darwin and is very much steeped in some of his ideas that are coming to the fore in his day. But it's also an idea that has a very long history in philosophy, where philosophers tend to think of themselves as among the few greats. In Plato, it's always the few against the many. We're not concerned with the many. We're concerned with the few who can do great things. In the *Republic*, Socrates says that only a great nature can be exceptionally good or exceptionally bad. The greatest natured people with the greatest capacity to do amazing things also have the greatest capacity to do atrocious things. Nietzsche's concern is that if you hold down people who are capable of great evil, you do so at the expense of people who are capable of great good. He thinks we're making a tradeoff and doing so unreflectively. Our very worldviews, built on this all-pervasive slave morality, have that tradeoff built into them. So, it's by default that we are sacrificing potential greatness to avoid potential dangers. But for Nietzsche, someone who can do really great things, even if they're terrible, is awe-inspiring and has the potential to make life worth living. He wants humanity to want to strive for something more than just mediocrity.

Orna: *What does Nietzsche think are the conditions for the possibility of someone having this capacity for greatness?*

Well, he certainly thinks that he himself has this capacity, which is not surprising. But I think we can look to Plato for an answer, and because Nietzsche was so heavily influenced by Plato, it will give us some insight. First, you have to be the type of person who is not satisfied with things as they are. The world as it is given to you is unsatisfactory, and you think you could make it better or do things differently. There's both a desire for things to be different and a belief that you're capable of making them different. And second, Plato says that if this type of person arises in the wrong setting, he will either be held down by the herd mentality or will be sent in the direction of doing terrible things instead of good things. Which is to say, the second condition is an environment or community that can foster greatness.

Lyn: *Could you speak to the relationship between this text and psychoanalysis in practice—that is, more explicitly, how might Nietzsche's philosophy take shape in the clinical interaction?*

Absolutely—some of the payoff from these ideas comes from the attempt to understand morality. On a deep psychological level, we all live under this type of morality of resentment but are unaware of it. We are brought up in a world that teaches us to understand ourselves as being less capable than we really are and to desire less the things that might make our lives worth living. Recall from *Birth* that Nietzsche sees art as something that can save us from psychosis. We become artists of our own lives when we can tell our story in a compelling way and this allows us to make sense out of our traumas by weaving them into a narrative. It gives us back a sense of control and agency over our own lives and stories. It helps us process and understand. Of course, it's all fiction. But that doesn't diminish the value of doing it.

Another valuable component of living artistically is the desire to always be better: the desire to tell a better story and to make our lives better. Living a more interesting life makes us love our lives the way we love great stories. So, it allows us to think of ourselves as capable of greatness. But we live in a world with a value system that teaches us it's better to be more like everyone else, less like ourselves, to have a less compelling story, and not to stand out. We don't value having more nuanced experiences that conflict with other peoples'. We're taught that there's something wrong if one should want to be a completely original person who does unique things and isn't satisfied with the status quo. You know, I hear from former students—and it's always the economics majors—who tell me that they're working 60 hours a week and they hate their jobs and are profoundly unfulfilled. They believed that they weren't capable of doing anything else, anything they valued more; they believed that ticking off boxes on a society-approved "list of things that make you successful" was what would lead to a fulfilling life. The stories we tell ourselves, rooted in our values, are incredibly powerful, and I think that's an insight with major clinical import.

David: *I'm reminded of David Schnarch's book,* Constructing the Sexual Crucible, *in which he argues that couples often kill intimacy by going for other-validated intimacy versus self-validated intimacy. In other words, they give up their own desires and essentially give up themselves in the interest of being selfless. They want to reduce conflict in the relationship, but this inadvertently kills passion.*

That's a fantastic example of another key clinical takeaway. If your focus is always outward, trying to please others and be selfless, then you don't have satisfaction in what you're striving for in your own life. And you lose essential aspects of yourself. Passion in a relationship is one such aspect. But this is a point Dostoevsky makes as well, and Nietzsche was a great reader of Dostoevsky. In *The Brothers Karamazov*, there's a woman who is ready to spend her whole life giving to others, yet she realizes that she always winds up resenting the people she helps. She resents them because they aren't grateful to her. And the character she's speaking with, Father Zosima, tells her that the people who need her help will never be grateful, that they're the most ungrateful people. He asks her why she is seeking their gratitude at all. And the woman realizes that she's always seeking meaning and approval externally instead of doing what would really be fulfilling to her internally. So, yes, selflessness can breed resentment and cause a person to lose sight of himself.

Jason: This makes me think about patients or clients who are very passive-aggressive in the clinical setting. They tend to be people who have been traumatized or subjugated by a beast of one sort or another—somebody who has oppressed them either physically or psychologically or both—because of their weakness. They had no way to defend themselves. What they have is their weakness and passivity, so they turn those into weapons that become their go-to weapons. And in the world beyond the beast who has abused them, they bring that passive aggression with them.

Another excellent point. And the problem is that weakness dressed up as strength is not actually strength, right? It actually hurts the passive-aggressive person more. For Nietzsche, one of the major problems with resentment is that to have resentment is to poison oneself. The man of resentment is a nihilist, which means that he hates life and doesn't want to be alive. So, if you're living in resentment and always seeing evil in others and using that to catalyze your own understanding of goodness, you're actually poisoning your understanding of the good. And that leads to a lot of dissatisfaction and misery.

Jason: One other observation I have is, it seems to me that Nietzsche is not a democrat, not an egalitarian. That is, he does not see the potential he's talking about in everyone. On the contrary, he says that the strength he's talking about is exceptional and only in the very few. The vast majority of people are going to be completely unable to do what he's talking about.

Yes, I think you're right, and in that way, he's very much like many of the major thinkers in the history of philosophy. They're often concerned with the value of the few. But for me, and this is why I like to teach these ideas to undergraduates, I could have anyone walk into the classroom and press him to ask himself what he thinks is valuable, what makes life worth living. It's not because everyone can be a world-historic writer or thinker, but because everyone to various degrees is capable of pushing toward and striving toward something he actually values. If you can question yourself and why you're doing what you're doing, you can orient yourself toward things you find meaningful. And in that way, you move toward living the ideal Nietzsche is putting forth. Or, at the very least, you will be less resentful.

When I'm writing and have a goal in mind, psychologically I'm in a very good way. I have something I'm striving toward. But when I finish a project, I'm a mess. I start looking at what other people are writing and where they're publishing, and I wonder why I'm not publishing with those same presses or why my books aren't getting as many ratings on Amazon. I become resentful. So, the payoff for me is not that I might rise to meet Nietzsche's ideal and change the world, but that I'm capable of striving toward something and pushing myself to be better. And I'm doing things that align with my own values and am less concerned with what other people value. I think this is a good, healthy virtue that Nietzsche opens for us.

Andrew: *I think maybe I disagree slightly. I agree that the act of striving toward something you value is affirming, but I also think that when you see somebody else who is better than you, and you can recognize the talent in that person and the greatness in their work, it doesn't necessarily breed resentment. Because you're so in love with that thing—be it writing or whatever—you appreciate and respect and value their work for its intrinsic goodness or beauty. So, in that sense as well, even if you aren't one of the few destined for greatness yourself, Nietzsche's ideas here are still valuable.*

It's a really fine point and something about which I think Nietzsche would agree. It benefits all of us to see human greatness and accomplishments on display. Going to the Vatican and seeing what people have been capable of doing in painting and sculpture and architecture—it's awe-inspiring. A good friend of mine likes to say that Miles Davis's *Kind of Blue* justifies existence. For him, it makes up for all the bad and all the suffering in the world. In Nietzschean terms, great works of art intoxicate and entice you back to life. Even if you know that you could never do such things, still they inspire you and make you want to keep living and being human. There's a sort-of pride in just being part of the human race.

Suzanne: *I'm thinking about what we said earlier about Darwin … It doesn't seem like Nietzsche has a progressive narrative. Although this is a common misconception about evolution as well—that it is progressive in the sense of improving upon itself, or that it has a telos. Does Nietzsche believe in progress?*

No, he doesn't. He doesn't think of history as progressive. In my reading of him, he thinks history is cyclical in a lot of ways. We're repeating the same patterns again and again. And it's cyclical in the sense that a certain value system can take us to a high point only to start leveling off and even beginning to diminish us. And this repeats with each new revolution in our value system. His goal, I think, is to challenge us to always be reinventing and reimagining what it is to be a human being. That way, when we start to diminish, we're prepared to take up the task of redefining our values and redefining ourselves again. He thinks of this as a never-ending cycle. In *Beyond Good and Evil*, he talks of his (our) time as one of sickness. Humans are sick with morality, sick with the moral system in which we live. And yet, we're sick as pregnancy is a sickness, in that it can open up to something new. It's the idea that, for instance, in the fall of Rome, there's immense possibility of something new being born into the world out of the chaos of Rome's demise. So, it's not a straight, linear, progressive narrative at least.

Orna: *It seems like Nietzsche's view of subjectivity, that there are all these perspectives and different interpretations and such, is really fundamental to his idea of reinvention, so that when you find yourself at a dead end, you have the ability to invent a way out by changing the narrative. Does that make sense?*

Yes, it's an excellent insight. As you say, Nietzsche is a perspectivist, meaning that he doesn't think we ever have some sort of ultimate access to an objective truth. We just have the cacophony of different perspectives that humans bring to a given situation. But, tying back to *The Birth of Tragedy*, the fact that so much of human life (perhaps all of it) is artifice, invention, construction, while terrifying and in some ways problematic, can be a very freeing thing. Because there's no bottom, no truth to rest upon, there's always the possibility to reinvent and do something completely new. You just have to realize that the morality and mentality other people take for granted and try to force on you is artifice. *No, you don't have to think that way and be that way. No, that isn't just the way the world is.* It frees you to reject the dominant perspective. And that will be a dangerous thing to do both for yourself and for your community. It's a precarious position. But that precariousness opens up the possibility for something new and great to arise.

3 Third Meeting, 03/31/2022

Bad Conscience: Whence the Super-Ego?

In the first essay of *On the Genealogy of Morals*, Nietzsche asks us to consider why we value what we value. As we said last time, he sees *ressentiment* as that which undergirds our moral ideals. That is, he sees in our values the desire to hold down and oppress those who are stronger than us, those exceptional few whose mere existence ought to give rise to exaltation. In his second essay, Nietzsche takes these ideas and applies them to the deeper psychological questions of how such values shape our subjectivities and why the human condition gives rise to them in the first place. For him, it is not only modern, liberal, democratic society that is rooted in the values and ethics of resentment, but society writ large. To live in society, to be a socialized creature, is to live under the sign of *ressentiment*, to be filled with animus for the beast we find in others and within ourselves. But what follows from this hostility to the essential characteristics of human life?

To broach this question, Nietzsche begins by pointing out something that, perhaps ironically, we often forget: the value of forgetting. The capacity of forgetfulness, he argues, is the hallmark of sentient life. If we were condemned to an existence of perpetual remembering, the traumas and sufferings we've incurred would overwhelm us and it would become impossible to live. An example may help to illustrate the point: A few years ago, I was pulling out of a parking lot onto the main street in the town in which I lived, and I saw a car coming toward me from the left. Its blinker was on. It was going to turn right onto the road just before the parking lot. That provided me with the gap in traffic I needed to pull out. What I didn't realize was that the driver of the other car was an elderly man who had mistakenly left his turn signal on. I assumed the Apollonian order of existence and had the veil ripped from my eyes when, as I was making my turn, he continued driving and tore the front clean off my car. Had I been just a foot further into my turn, he would have hit my driver's side door and perhaps maimed or killed me. Luckily, neither of us was hurt, but of course, both of our cars were totaled. Once things calmed down, I called my wife and she came to pick me up. At the time, we had just had our first son, so he was with her. Seeing the wreck and knowing that I might have been killed upset her immensely. She was really shaken and

DOI: 10.4324/9781003348795-3

asked me if I could drive us home. So I got into her car with my wife and our new baby, got on the freeway, and drove home as if nothing had happened. I didn't think about the accident again until I had to contact the insurance company later that afternoon.

Moments after the crash, it naturally occurred to me that I had almost died. I felt lucky to walk away unscathed. But if that thought had remained with me, I wouldn't have been able to drive home. I wouldn't have been able to go on with my life. Instead, I forgot the trauma almost immediately. Or, if I remembered it, it became an abstraction, a thought that removed me from the experience itself. Because of this, I was able to do what needed to be done. I could tend to my wife's shock and take care of my family. It is in this way, Nietzsche says, that forgetting plays an essential role in our lives. As we saw in the first essay, those who don't forget become resentful. It is the remembrance of past wrongs that breeds resentment. We hold onto the times we have been disappointed, disillusioned, and hurt, and refuse to get beyond them. A healthier constitution would forget, Nietzsche says. Or better still, a healthier mind would overcome the frustration in order to move on. Slights sting so long as we let them. Psychologically, then, the ability to forget is an immensely important character trait. It is a sign of vigor and good health.

But for Nietzsche, forgetfulness is only half the equation. Its reverse, the capacity to remember, is just as psychologically significant. The fact that we can resist the very forgetfulness that is so beneficial to us, that we can stem the flow of time by bringing the past into the present and projecting it forward into the future, is for Nietzsche one of man's crowning achievements. It marks a major psychological development, one that demands attention. Memory, Nietzsche says, makes possible all of human life. It is responsible, for example, for my being here tonight—I made a commitment to do so and, in spite of all the things that have happened since we last met, my memory has served to preserve that commitment in my mind and helped me to ensure that I would fulfill my obligation. So much of human life relies upon this faculty, and is rooted in it. Without memory, man could not live.

This realization, however, gives Nietzsche pause. We just said that life is better, our constitutions healthier, when we forget the traumas and the pain of existence. We just said that memory stifles action, causes anxiety, and makes life unlivable. Yet human beings are the remembering animal. Where does this tension come from? Why did it develop?

Jason: *I'm reminded of a short story by Jorge Luis Borges called "Funes the Memorious" about a man who cannot forget anything, ever. He remembers every single thing he experiences, and he ends up as this paralyzed, tragic figure. I'd highly recommend it.*

Who is better than JLB? That plot is almost the exact opposite of the Christopher Nolan movie *Memento* about a character who has no memory.

He is seeking revenge for a wrong he doesn't quite remember. Obviously, his forgetfulness gets in his way, and he is really unable to function in society. But on the other hand, he is able to vent his anger, be done with it, and move forward, so he actually has a fairly healthy constitution. Anyway, this is the very tension that Nietzsche is exploring in this second essay: We are these strange creatures with the capacity to remember, in opposition to what is good for us, which is to forget. He wants to understand why memory arose in the first place. It must meet some need or offer some benefit in spite of its many drawbacks. Social life, he thinks, is the main beneficiary of this capacity and, indeed, society is the context in which memory first arises and becomes useful.

Civilization, Nietzsche thinks, hangs upon memory. This is clear if we consider how we are able to live and work in relation to one another, to do our jobs and fulfill our commitments, to organize ourselves into social units and build upon the achievements of past generations. In order to do any of the things civilization requires us to do, we have to become calculable animals—dependable, regulated, regimented. Collective life becomes easier the more structure is imposed upon each life individually. Without that dependability, we would have no way of maintaining an orderly, well-functioning society. And memory is that which ensures dependability and makes it possible for us to bring structure to life.

Although memory is a necessary part of communal life, it does not, Nietzsche thinks, arise accidentally. It is, rather, created by force, evoked from without, imposed upon us the way I impose order upon my dog. According to Nietzsche's genealogy, citizens in the first community were herded together into a populace by those who were stronger, those with the power to exert their vision of humanity onto the yet unformed masses. These early artiests of human nature forced their inferiors to become orderly and regimented. (This imagined genesis of social life is not so different from the picture Freud offers in *Totem and Taboo*. There, he invents a story of origin for the human community that is also based on the weak (women and children, in particular) submitting to the brute force of the strong (the Oedipal father).) For Nietzsche, the earliest human beings were nomadic "semi-animals," cultivated apes who were forced by threat of violence to move into collective life because it was to the benefit of the strong to make them do so. And this, he thinks, is the building block of the whole history of human civilization.

But how do you cultivate order, regularity, and reliability in a chaotic mass of animals? How do you instill the capacity for memory? Nietzsche says that these first social planners did so in the exact same way that parents impose order upon their children—they used the threat of violence. If you want people to remember something, he says, you show them what will happen to them if they don't. For Nietzsche, violence is a mnemonic device. There is no more potent stimulant for memory. (We understand this intuitively when we say something has been "burned" into our heads.) In parenting, there has been a movement away from this kind of corporal punishment.

But the threat of a negative outcome—taking something away, for instance, or putting a child in timeout, or having him lose certain privileges—has a similar, if less acute, violence to it.

Again, think of how we train domesticated animals. My family recently got a dog, a golden retriever named Joey, and in order to train him not to jump on people or eat food off the table, we bought a shock collar. The collar itself is an instrument of violence—any collar is. Think of what it communicates, wrapped tightly around the throat. It says, "you are not free, obey or you will be choked." But this collar is more menacing than most. It makes a beeping noise if the dog's owner presses a button on the remote control that comes with it. That provides an auditory warning for him to stop the unwanted behavior. If he doesn't stop, we press the button again and the collar vibrates. That's a second warning, another threat of violence. If he continues to misbehave at that point, we press a different button and it gives him a little shock. We have only ever had to shock Joey maybe twice. Now, just having the collar on is enough to prevent him from jumping on the table. Now, he remembers what not to do. So it is really the threat of violence more so than violence itself that helps us to train and maintain certain behaviors. And this, Nietzsche thinks, is at the foundation of social life. We follow laws, we do our jobs, we act like good, moral citizens, all because we fear being shocked. We too wear the collar around our necks. We too remember what behaviors will be punished.

Nietzsche points out that throughout history, rulers have made a show of punishment and violence—public executions and displays of torture, public shaming, character assassination, and so on. That is because making an example out of the few is enough to scare the many into submission. (What possible reason could there be for tarring and feathering besides signaling to the masses the fate that awaits them if they step out of line?) These often horrific and absurd displays of violence sear into our collective memory a few "I will nots"—what rules and norms must not be violated. But pain and punishment are more complicated still. Not only are they useful tools for cultivating memory and deterring unwanted behavior, they also provide a good deal of pleasure to those who get to inflict the punishment. This is the second important insight into human psychology offered by this section of *Genealogy*—human beings are fundamentally sadistic creatures.

It was the desire to inflict pain, Nietzsche tells us, that inspired the strong to herd the masses into collective life and form the earliest societies. The will to overpower and overcome resistances, to dominate and subdue, is an essential part of life—perhaps *the* essential part of life, according to Nietzsche. Thus it ought not to surprise us that the human herd, once domesticated and punished into obedience, should also express a desire to inflict suffering on others. And so, it's not just that the subjected don't like to be punished. They—*we*—are the same kind of animal as the strong, made from the same stock, harboring the same instincts and cruelty, desiring to drink in another's pain in just the same way. The only difference is our capacity to do so. We are restrained by the confines of society. But that doesn't mean our desire is any less potent; if anything, it is heightened. We must simply find other means of satisfying it, subtle detours that take us to the same end.

One such means is the institution of the relationship between the creditor and the debtor. The dynamic between the one who lends and expects repayment and the one who owes and must repay is, according to Nietzsche, at the very foundation of social life as well. Once the capacity for memory has been forged into the human animal, we become able to remember our promises and can thus be expected to repay our debts. As a trained philologist, Nietzsche traces this dynamic through ancient languages and ancient texts. It is something that we find built into the very words and categories we use to describe our relations. (How often do we say things like "I *owe* her a phone call" or "I'm going to *pay* him a visit" or "I'm *indebted* to you" or "We can *credit* her with that" and so on?) And in this creditor/debtor dynamic, the power play of punisher and punished that we find on a societal level can be carried out on a smaller, individual scale. It offers the prospects of being able to satisfy one's desire for cruelty in a socially sanctioned way. For, when the debtor is unable to pay his debt, the creditor receives not an equal payment, but the pleasure of being able to inflict punishment upon him. *That* is the benefit to the creditor in this dynamic, the license to cause harm.

Nietzsche points to the history of debtors being tortured and humiliated in public, and this idea of taking a "pound of flesh" as payment for a defaulted debt. In Shakespeare's *The Merchant of Venice*, for example, when Antonio fails to pay back what he owes, Shylock demands satisfaction in the flesh. This play is not some relic from the ancient world. It was written a mere four hundred years ago, and such a demand made sense to audiences back then. It makes sense to us today. That is because, according to Nietzsche, this dynamic is merely an extension of and means of satisfying an underlying aspect of the human psyche—the lust for cruelty. We are fundamentally sadistic. And society gives some of us the ability to vent our frustrations, fantasies, and lusts on others.

Nietzsche writes,

> To see others suffer does one good, to make others suffer even more: this is a hard saying but an ancient, mighty, human, all-too-human principle to which even the apes might subscribe; for it has been said that in devising bizarre cruelties they anticipate man and are, as it were, his "prelude." Without cruelty there is no festival: thus the longest and most ancient part of human history teaches—and in punishment there is so much that is *festive*! (GM, 2, §6)

We read this and recoil. If we stop and consider, however, we will have to admit that Nietzsche is right. Consider comedy, for instance. Take *Don*

Quixote. In Cervantes' masterwork, the humor is in its cruelty. What we laugh at is this poor, dumb sot who keeps getting hurt or making a fool out of himself. We laugh because we can ridicule. We can enjoy his pain. Again, in Shakespearean comedies and tragedies, there is always the part of the fool, the jester whose sole purpose is to be mocked and debased. There's a pleasure, a joy even, in being able to vent our sadistic desires on others. Comedy today functions along the same lines. It's only funny if someone is hurt.

For Nietzsche, this aspect of human psychology is ever present, but as we progress as a society and become more civilized, more domesticated, it is sublimated into subtler and subtler forms. The more refined we are, the more we spiritualize our sadism. It becomes less visceral, less visible, and thus less apparent to us, but it does not go away. We begin to understand our relationship to society itself along the same lines as that between the debtor and the creditor. We see ourselves in the role of debtor to society writ large, which in turn becomes our creditor.

In one of Plato's dialogues, the *Crito*, Socrates refuses to take advantage of an opportunity to escape from prison and instead accepts his fate after being sentenced to death. Socrates tells Crito that to escape would be unjust, not because he is guilty of the charges levied against him, but because of what he owes to the city of Athens. He reasons that without Athens, his parents would never have been married and never would have conceived him. He wouldn't have the clothes on his back or have had an education, access to food, shelter, and so on. All the benefits of society had been bestowed upon him by the city, and therefore he is in the position of the debtor in relation to the state. He says that since the city has determined he must die, he is obligated to follow its edict. He owes the city that much. For Nietzsche, all of us, perhaps unconsciously, adopt a similar view of our relation to the societies in which we live. We see ourselves as benefactors who bear the weight of an unpayable debt, a commitment to our creditor—the state—that binds us and forces us to live like caged animals, obligated to follow the rules and regulations imposed on us from without and be "good citizens," that is, dutiful borrowers who continue to pay interest on what is owed. There is a disparity between the state and the individual, a gulf between the creditor and the debtor that can never be overcome.

It is this imbalance that leads individual persons to form what Nietzsche calls "bad conscience." Bad conscience is the individual's desire to vent his animal anger, his natural drive to overpower others, combined with his impotency, his inability to do so. In Freudian terms, it is a neurosis, and all civilized life is sick. We are sick because what we want most we cannot have. We are restrained from pursuing our most basic desires and thus alienated from ourselves. What we do in response is what the caged animal does. We develop the neurosis of rubbing up against the bars. We develop a bad conscience that, unable to be vented outward, directs its venom inward and poisons the self.

To give another anecdote from my life: When my oldest son was around three, my wife and I first started to institute timeouts for bad behavior, particularly when he hit his younger brother with a toy. Naturally, we tried to prevent such behavior in advance by talking to him about it and about the consequences of his actions. But, at those times when no amount of forewarning deterred him and he did hit his brother, we would put him in timeout for three minutes. As he sat there, unable to vent his fury, he would turn it in on himself and start hitting himself on the head, which was a really painful thing to see. It's horrible, but this is Nietzsche's insight: if we can't discharge our cruelty outwardly by inflicting it on others, the pent-up anger has to go somewhere, and we will thus turn it in on ourselves. This is Freud's point as well—neurosis is an illness we choose because it's preferable to be sick than to admit to ourselves that we have malicious desires. And Nietzsche thinks that this is characteristic of us all; we're all neurotic in some way because we are forced to live as debtors under the creditor of the state, which alone has the license to enjoy its violence.

This understanding of bad conscience is, I believe, the foundation for the Freudian superego. Not only do we become neurotic in venting our frustration inward because we cannot do so outwardly, but we also adopt the punishments of society—the rules, restrictions, and regulations—as our own internal laws. We check our own behavior and become the watchmen of ourselves, policing our psyches the way the state polices our actions. In this way, bad conscience gives way to guilty conscience. Not only is my anger directed inward, but I now say I deserve to have my anger turned inward because I am guilty. I am a debtor before a creditor I can never repay. And this occurs in religion as well, where we project the idealized creditor onto God. We are completely guilty before God, never able to repay our debts, and deserving of his punishment and ire.

David: *That's really the essence of traditional Christian theology, isn't it? I'm thinking of the hymn we used to sing in church: "O to grace how great a debtor daily I'm constrained to be. Let that grace, Lord, like a fetter, bind my wandering heart to thee." Then again, in some theories of atonement, the debt is somehow repaid and satisfied through Christ's death on the cross.*

Yes, Nietzsche, as the son of a Lutheran pastor, was very much informed by themes and aspects of Christian theology like this. We are so indebted to God that he had to send his own son as ransom for us to pay off the debt that we could never repay ourselves. But actually, what's really interesting in this example is that religion makes you all the more guilty, because now you're indebted all the more to the son whose sacrifice paid the first debt. You aren't really relieved of debt, it's shifted to a new creditor. You've become more and more unworthy and in need of punishment and so on.

A.M. Pelos: *It's like with student loan forgiveness. If the government forgives some of that debt, although I'm less in debt on paper, doesn't my debt to society—to every American taxpayer, but also to the institutions of government, perhaps even to the Democratic party and to President Biden himself—actually increase? I'll feel all the more guilty, and this whole system and psychology is only reinforced.*

Yes, that's an excellent example. And in that way, bad conscience becomes an incredibly useful tool in the hands of politicians who rely upon your guilt to buy your vote. For Nietzsche, this psychology—to return to the first essay—is rooted in the Judeo-Christian value system of good and evil. Whereas resentment is the passive-aggressive attempt to punish others by restraining them in response to their being in positions of power, bad conscience is our self-inflicted punishment. We feel guilty and punish ourselves. We are unable to accept ourselves as we are, and again, this ties into the religious element of despising the corporeal body. The spiritualization of cruelty means that we hate ourselves not only internally, in our psyches, but we come to despise our bodies as the vessels responsible for our "impure" desires. We become disgusted with bodily existence and seek to deny our nature. We say, "I am not my body, but my soul." Nietzsche is pointing out that we are animals that can't accept being animals—physical, desiring, chaotic bundles of drives. We cannot accept our sadism and our lust and all of the things that go along with our carnality.

Lyn: *When he discusses these dynamics, is it purely descriptive? Or is there any outrage or judgment on Nietzsche's part? Also, in some ways, this sounds very German to me—how much of this is culturally rooted in a certain time and place?*

I read Nietzsche as primarily descriptive rather than trying to offer his own kind of normative morality. On the surface, it doesn't necessarily seem that way. He's very polemical and has a dark sort of humor. I think he's often making himself into a bit of a caricature in order to be provocative and awaken us to forgotten or neglected truths. He says of himself, "I am no man, I am dynamite" (EH, "Why I am a Destiny," §1) and he certainly writes that way. But if these things are missed, it can be easy to overstate the significance of his advocacy. I do think he's diagnosing the state of affairs as best as he can and he highlights how horrifying these things really are. Then in the next breath, he'll say that nevertheless, these very same problems offer us enormous benefits, and there are many ways they help us. So he tries to view whatever subject he is examining from as many angles as he possibly can, which to me is the work of a good investigator.

In terms of his cultural context, Nietzsche is absolutely a German thinker and responding to movements in German idealism and to other German philosophers at the time. And of course, he is a perspectivist, which means he thinks there is no culturally detached or disinterested philosophy. He says, for instance, that all philosophy is really an autobiography. That is, one's philosophy is one's understanding of the world and one's relation to it. And in the preface to *Genealogy,* he says that he had these questions at thirteen years old and now in his thirties is finally coming to some answers. So all writing is personal for Nietzsche and this work is no exception. That said, he is an expert philologist (at only twenty-four, before even finishing his PhD, he was given a full professorship because he was considered to be a genius in philology) who studies ancient languages and cultures, and he believes he is identifying things that track across different places and times. Ultimately, I think we have to read Nietzsche as fundamentally rooted in his time and place, but I think he believes he is accounting for something common to all humanity.

Lyn: *Do you think he's also angry? I mean, you mentioned his humorous side, but there seems to be some deep anger underlying his philosophy. And you know, if I ever come to your house for dinner, please don't zap me!*

We make all guests remove their shoes and put on shock collars when they enter, so don't expect an invite any time soon. But I think you're right. Nietzsche would say that if we're being honest with ourselves, we'll all recognize the anger and resentment we harbor within. But it's hard to be honest. It's hard to look into that mirror. We don't like the face we see looking back. So he definitely can come across as angry—he doesn't exclude himself from his analysis. But when I read him, I tend to find someone who forces me to examine my own flaws. I hear my own meanness coming through in his words. On the other hand, Nietzsche was close friends with Wagner and for a time wanted to be a composer himself. He wrote his own music, but he was no Wagner, and you can see a turn in his writing where he goes from praising Wagner's genius to completely trashing and attacking him. So, I think it's clear in his life that he isn't immune to *ressentiment,* and he is aware of this—the same way that Freud would say he himself is a hysteric.

Now, as Lyn suggests, this can all seem rather pessimistic. But Nietzsche will not leave us without offering a glimpse of hope. In the first seminar, we discussed how he points out in *Birth of Tragedy* that in order for there to be the possibility of hope, for life beyond trauma, we have to be first and foremost brutally honest and pessimistic about the way life presents itself. That extreme pessimism can open paradoxically onto something very hopeful and joyful. At the same time, as he gives us a somewhat nihilistic worldview, he wants to resist nihilism. He wants us to see through to the deepest abysses of human existence, to delve deeper into the crevasse, so that we might find a way out the other side—a way to something new.

Although humans are characterized by bad conscience, and this is due to the development of memory by which we become resentful and self-loathing, at the same time, memory provides us with incredible opportunities and possibilities for the human species. As the last links in a long chain of cruelty and repression and neurosis, we might see ourselves as the heirs and beneficiaries of that history—we might harness it and develop, in place of bad conscience, liberated conscience, free conscience, true autonomy. Remember, bad conscience arises because we adhere to certain rules under the threat of punishment. It comes out of the weaponization of memory against us. In contrast, liberated conscience is the use of our capacity for memory to keep our commitments out of a desire to do so and not for any external reasons. Nietzsche thinks this is the greatest possibility for human beings—to stand good on our promises for our own security and the security of those we care about, not to take our commitments lightly. Someone who keeps promises not out of fear of the repercussions for breaking them but out of his own integrity, Nietzsche says, does so as a sovereign individual. A sovereign individual does not live under the oppression of morality and the fear of punishment. A sovereign individual lives out of commitment to himself, a deep and abiding integrity that no one can take away.

But this idea, I think, extends beyond the everyday commitments and interpersonal promises we make. Nietzsche has in mind the possibility of someone aspiring to do something truly brilliant with his life. Whenever one aspires to greatness, all sorts of obstacles will inevitably get in one's way. When they do, it can be really easy to lose sight of one's aspirations and make excuses. But the sovereign individual will not forget the promise he has made to himself. What Nietzsche admires most in humans is the capacity to overcome obstacles, to face adversity and forge ahead. What he wants is for us to remember the promises we make to ourselves and not give up on them. He says early in the second essay, "the emancipated individual, with the actual *right* to make promises, this master of a *free* will [is a] sovereign man" (GM, 2, §2). He also says that this person has an immense responsibility:

> The proud awareness of the extraordinary privilege of responsibility, the consciousness of this rare freedom, this power over oneself and over fate, has in his case penetrated to the profoundest depths and become instinct, the dominating instinct. What will he call this dominating instinct, supposing he feels the need to give it a name? The answer is beyond doubt: this sovereign man calls it his *conscience*. (GM, 2, §2)

Thus, Nietzsche tells us that conscience can be restored from the place of bad conscience to a fully robust and authentic human conscience—one defined by and committed to the standard it sets for itself, rather than the standard imposed upon it from without.

❖

David: *That sounds lovely and all, but given everything we've just been saying, it seems like quite a leap. What would Nietzsche say about how someone could get to that place?*

Well, I think he believes you can't get there without first seeing things for what they really are—that is, admitting the monstrous parts of life that we usually gloss over or cloak in euphemisms in order to look the other way. So everything we've been saying is an important part of getting to that point. You have to realize that your guilt and shame about your body and your desires and your malice and so forth are the results of social prohibitions and the internalization of punishment. If you don't see morality as this type of social tool, then you'll never be free of those chains that bind you. But again, I think Nietzsche is very much an elitist who doesn't believe that everyone can (or ought to) do this, at least not in the way he envisions. The sovereign is a very rare person for him, and it takes a rare constitution to both understand psychology in this way and be able to convert desire into a necessity, as when he talks about the dominating instinct. He has in mind someone who is capable of taking what he wants and turning it into what he needs. It's taking a vision one has for oneself and by sheer will conjuring it, so to speak, into reality.

Jason: *In terms of what he may be prescribing, it sounds very similar to Freud: We have instincts—that is, the libido or the Id—that are regulated by society and an internalized regimentation that threaten us with punishment—that is, the superego. And under that model, we keep promises out of fear of retribution. But if we can get rid of that internal regulation and instead make promises from a place of instinct, or out of desires we are driven toward but not forced into, then we might free ourselves of bad conscience, or our neuroses.*

Yes, that's a helpful analogy. Nietzsche calls it free will, though it's not a concept of free will like any traditional philosopher I can think of. But it is will that is free of the oppression of the master and the superego. And it's an authentic, instinctual will—the will to power reflects the deepest desires we have.

Jason: *And it recalls the idea of the Dionysian drive as well—coming more from within than from without.*

Right. It's the difference he notes in the first essay between the person of *ressentiment* who is defined by his reaction to others—his fear or envy of someone else—and the person who is self-driven and self-affirming.

Suzanne: *I can't help but read this through lenses of gender and race; I'm trying to be generous with Nietzsche, but his ideas seem rather Eurocentric to me. It's a sort-of language of privilege that he's speaking with and I'm wondering what your thoughts are on that.*

There's no doubt that there's something very masculine in his understanding and interpretation of society here. I think in part this is because Nietzsche's view of society itself is that it is fundamentally masculine—in the sense of being oppressive and characterized by sadism. Masculinity, the libido, and sadism are all connected for Freud and for Nietzsche as well. But his prescription at the end is also a masculine response to the problem. We'll see in *Beyond Good and Evil* that his ideas on gender are more nuanced. For instance, he conceives of truth as essentially feminine, and he says that a lover of truth should try to mirror that femininity and not try to grasp it and possess it in a masculine way, the way most philosophers do. He even accuses his fellow philosophers of being hypermasculine and thus not approaching truth with the proper disposition. But your point about his Eurocentrism is apt. He went to the best schools and is highly educated and privileged. He is certainly writing from a particular perspective and with a particular worldview. He never denies this. In many ways, his work made possible the contemporary critiques of critical theorists. Before Nietzsche, the truth was Truth, and when philosophers made claims, they were arguing about what they believed to be universally valid for all human beings. It's Nietzsche's perspectivism that paves the way for the insights of gender and cultural theorists who say, "Wait a second, let's not merely consider the ideas but the perspective of the person behind the ideas."

Lyn: *One thing that's coming up for me here is the idea that perhaps only the educated and cultured kind of man can transcend the envy and resentment and become the sovereign individual, and I'm curious as to your thoughts on that.*

I think that, actually, not only is being cultured not a prerequisite for this kind of sovereignty, but it is really detrimental to it. That is, the more cultured and civilized you are, the more likely you are to be neurotic, to have a strong superego, to be filled with *ressentiment*, and so forth because these things are indoctrinated through education. For Nietzsche, the more plebeian person is less resentful because he is often more willing to give into a momentary fit of anger and enjoys more physical outlets for discharging his rage. In *Birth*, remember, the Dionysian is sexual and crude humor, dance, farce, drunkenness, letting oneself go. It's the opposite of refined culture. So, the sovereign individual will let go of a lot of culture and more closely resemble someone who is forgetful of manners and rules. Going back to where we started, it is the forgetful person who is most happy and innocent. The sovereign individual, then, can use memory selectively—to remember his commitments, but also to forget how others have wronged him.

David: I'm reminded also of the tortured philosophy of Augustine.

Nietzsche is very much responding to Augustine and Plato and the refined philosophy of the Stoics, for instance. There is a tendency among ancient and medieval philosophers to argue that giving up our basal instincts and focusing instead on abstract ideas, prioritizing the soul to the exclusion of the body, is the just and virtuous thing to do. But Nietzsche, again, emphasizing the feminine quality of truth, recognizes the bodily nature of human existence. The feminine qualities of being close to nature and partaking in violent births, for instance—these are closer to real life and to the heart of human existence than the abstractions of speculative philosophy.

David: And those neo-Platonic views really set the tone for Christian theology—this idea that the body is the prison of the soul.

Yes, it's fascinating to see how much a certain type of Platonism influenced the entire history of the west through Christianity. As descendants of that culture and beneficiaries of its doctrines, we still feel the aftershock today. Think of how much we hate the body, how we conceal and try to manipulate it and mask its appearance and odors and everything natural that goes along with it. Think of how we talk about the "true self" as the person within—we no longer use the word "soul," but the concept is as alive as ever. We say, "Don't judge a book by its cover" and mean "Don't judge a person by the body. It's what's inside that really counts."

Jean-Luc: Everyone knows the cover is the most important part of the book. Its appearance, how it looks and feels—even how it smells, the smell of the pages—drastically changes the reading experience. Appearance makes all the difference.

I couldn't agree more. My biggest gripe with most presses that publish philosophy is that they pump out these hideous books. Look at a catalog of recent philosophy titles and you'll see what I mean. You won't want to read any of them. … I just noticed Orna drinking a glass of wine, and I'm thinking I should pour myself one.

Orna: I had a really long day and just wanted to listen and enjoy today's session.

Now I'm thinking I should start our next session with a glass of whiskey. That would be very enjoyable. There's nothing wrong with that.

A.M. Pelos: It's a perfectly Dionysian thing to do, no?
Jason: Quite right.

4 Fourth Meeting, 04/28/2022

God Is Dead: Living in the Absence of the Father

This evening, you have the distinguished pleasure of spending my birthday with me. We don't really celebrate birthdays in my house, so this seminar is what I've been looking forward to all day. I can think of few ways I'd rather spend my birthday than talking about Nietzsche.

Before we get into *The Gay Science* and *Thus Spoke Zarathustra*, I want to draw your attention to a quotation from *Ecce Homo*, Nietzsche's autobiography. The phrase *"ecce homo"* is Latin for "behold the man" and is used by Pontius Pilate in the Vulgate translation of the Gospel of John to refer to Jesus. In appropriating this allusion and using it when exposing himself, Nietzsche is being comically self-aggrandizing. He weaves a lot of humor into his writing, which I think is an important and often overlooked aspect of his corpus. In the passage I want to quote, found in a chapter titled "Why I am so Wise," Nietzsche reflects on his own birth: "The good fortune of my existence, its uniqueness perhaps, lies in its fatality: I am, to express it in the form of a riddle, already dead as my father, while as my mother I am still living and becoming old" (EH, "Why I am so Wise," §1). Nietzsche's father, who, as I have mentioned before, was a Lutheran pastor, died when Nietzsche was only five years old, and it was assumed of Nietzsche that he would go on to take up the family business. In fact, he went to school to become a pastor and was very highly educated at a young age with that expectation in mind. But of course, he didn't ultimately become one, and so we have Nietzsche saying he's already died as his father—he's been his father and died to that life. And continuing in that vein, he says he is living out his mother's life. I wanted to begin by introducing this idea, but I'll leave it here for now and hope to return to it by the end.

I also want to briefly recall the role played by the father in Freud's developmental psychology. In *Totem and Taboo*, one of the driving questions for Freud is that of the origin of the religious impulse in human history. He sees that wherever there are human beings, there is religion. Morality, of course, arises in a religious context—we are always deifying our laws and customs—and civilization has religion as its cornerstone. So religion is foundational, or at least symptomatic of something foundational, for human beings. Freud begins *Totem and Taboo* by examining totemic religion, the

DOI: 10.4324/9781003348795-4

earliest expressions of man's religious life, and asking why it is that pre-historic man worships certain animals as sacred and why it becomes taboo to slaughter them. At times, Freud notices, there's a dispensation of the taboo, and religious devotees are allowed to kill and consume one of the sacred animals. In so doing, they express a kind of identification with the animal—the individual devotee is at one with the totem or god. But where does this behavior come from? What in us gives rise to the religious impulse in the first place?

About midway through the text, Freud looks to psychoanalysis for answers and realizes that child development may offer some insight. If you want to learn about the psychology of the earliest human beings, you don't have to study them directly—this is one of the remarkable real-izations of Freud. If you have little kids, you have prehistoric human beings living in your house, and you can observe them to learn what the earliest humans might have been like. The infancy of man is right there on display in infants today. Thus, Freud suggests that if we want to understand totemic religion, we should consider how children think about animals.

Going through various examples from his casework, Freud pays particular attention to the story of little Hans. Hans, who was four years old at the time, had a terrible phobia of horses, and Freud was trying to uncover what was behind it. As he talked to the boy, he began to realize that Hans har-bored a deep-seated dread of his father and a fear of the oppression of his father. Yet at the same time, there was an admiration for his father, a love for and idolization of his father in the boy's psyche. The ambivalence that existed within the child, Freud says, became so overwhelming that he ended up displacing his fear of his father onto horses. Horses became the substitute toward which he could express his angst. Now what's interesting about the fear that tormented the child is that, just like the ambivalence he felt toward his father, it was bound up with an intense love of horses and desire to be a horse. So these conflicting feelings are played out and allowed to express themselves at a distance, away from the father who is actually the monstrous and idolized object ravaging the boy's inner world.

In the context of totemic religion, Freud goes on to extrapolate, the love and hatred that gets displaced onto the animal is divinized, it becomes a god. Therefore, according to Freud, the fear of the father can be seen as the root cause of religion. In *Civilization and Its Discontents*, for instance, he writes:

> The derivation of religious needs from the infant's helplessness and the longing for the father aroused by it seems to me incontrovertible, especially since the feeling is not simply prolonged from childhood days, but is permanently sustained by fear of the superior power of Fate. I cannot think of any need in childhood as strong as the need for a father's protection. (CD, p. 20)

The origin of the religious attitude can be traced back to the feeling of infantile helplessness. And it's important to note the ambivalence associated with that helplessness. A child is at once completely in need of the father's protection and also helpless to oppose or resist the father's demands. This break within the child—the simultaneous dependence upon and fear of the father—as the child grows is ultimately projected onto God the father, the idealized father, the image of the father that has been sublimated into the religious sphere. For Freud, this idealized father plays a very important role in our lives. It is our sense of security, our source of meaning, and a way of orienting ourselves within the world. Having some sort of ideal—a god in the broadest sense—gives us an assurance that our lives mean something and a sense of right and wrong, a path to follow. It provides comfort and security and many other social and psychological benefits besides.

But what happens, of course, is that the father dies. In *Totem and Taboo*, Freud tells a myth, a sort of genesis narrative, in which the original father is killed by the very sons who revere him. They are oppressed by their father and have these ambivalent feelings toward him, so they band together as a tribe and murder him. But then they're left in this predicament of still having the ambivalent feelings, with the addition of remorse and guilt for having killed their own father. (Think of what we said about bad conscience and how it racks the psyche in our last meeting.) They have to live in the aftermath of that Oedipal origin, and the father's shadow still hangs over everything. The father, while dead, is not done away with. He cannot be simply forgotten.

Similarly, for Nietzsche, in the first essay of *Genealogy of Morals*, the history of human beings is such that the founders of any given society end up taking on the role of the creditor in relation to the next generation, who see themselves as indebted to the past. Even though those ancestors are now dead, their ghosts loom over everything. The ancestors become deified. In the United States, for instance, think about how we fetishize the American founding—the events, the documents, the "founding fathers" themselves. In any civilization, this is done collectively in a way very similar to what Freud sees as happening within the context of religion. We recognize our debt to our fathers—to previous generations—and they take on a sacred aura which strengthens their claims on our lives. As we said in our last meeting with respect to bad conscience and the superego, we internalize the rules of the father and make them our own, thereby becoming beings defined by our fathers, our ancestors, our idealized gods.

Of course, this happens, Nietzsche says, just as society begins to flourish. But the more a society rises in prominence, the more comfortable it becomes and the more comfortable its citizens are, the more the debt to their ancestors is forgotten. Nietzsche sees this loss of reverence for our ancestors as a sign of decadence. That is, as long as a society is on the rise, the ancestors loom large and occupy a prominent space in the collective psyche. But once a society is well-established, it starts to create its own customs and norms and starts to view its indebtedness to the past as oppressive. As a result, there is a backlash against the ancestors. Their sins begin to be revealed and they are no longer revered or deified. We can see this in American culture today with the questioning of the founding fathers and figures like Columbus and Lincoln who were once idolized as gods. We start to question them and the stories that we have been telling ourselves about them for so long, and suddenly they fall, not to the level of human beings, but often further still. We end up viewing them as subhuman monsters.

Nietzsche sees this as precisely the point of cultural development at which we modern human beings are living. We are just starting to reckon with the fact that our idealized God is insufficient, an undeity of our own making. Just as the sons in Freud's genesis myth have to grapple with the reality that they have killed their father, so we must grapple with our realization that "God is dead. God remains dead. And we have killed him" (GS, 3, §125). This is what the madman proclaims in tonight's reading from *The Gay Science*. In a later section, Nietzsche clarifies that the ramifications of this realization are just starting to be felt. We are just starting to feel the loss of our idol and cannot yet see the implications of it or what it will bring.

Nietzsche is often thought of as heralding in the death of God as some joyous event, ushering in the promise of a godless age. But that couldn't be further from what he says here. The death of God causes a profound disorientation. The idealized father, the law, the internal rules, the superego—these things have been taken into the self and have become a part of it. Even if they are oppressive, they provide a way of understanding oneself and the world and offer a path forward, a means of making it through the trials and terrors of life. As Camus says, bad answers are preferable to no answers at all. There's a sense of comfort and familiarity in knowing where things stand, even if that state of things is tyrannical and illusory. But when you start to lose the thing that orients you, gives you meaning, grounds your values, there is a sense of loss and even danger. The madman says that the world has become unchained from its sun. We no longer have something to orbit, something that gives us a sense of place. According to Nietzsche, this is a curse, the symptom of a profound sickness. But at the same time it represents a great opportunity. There is the sickness unto death and then there is "an illness as pregnancy is an illness" (GM, 2, §19), a poison that, if prescribed correctly, actually has the power to heal. At the very moment when we are becoming aware that our God—the idol of the father—is merely an illusion, an oppressive master we have set over ourselves, at the same time that we are losing that which gave our lives its meaning and provided a sense of security and stability, we are also being given the chance to respond to that awareness, to put our newfound knowledge toward some bettering ends. And these possible responses are what Nietzsche lays out in *Thus Spoke Zarathustra*.

The first response that we might have to this realization is psychological, and it's a response that I think is common in our world today. Nietzsche calls it the response of the last man. The last man is the modern malaise: it's the loss of the sense of ultimate meaning without any notion of what can replace it, what should be done, or even any real consideration or concern over the dilemma we now face. Returning to *Genealogy*, it's the way in which we continue to assume Judeo-Christian values—rooted in *ressentiment*, leveling greatness down to mediocrity, reactionary to the stronger, etc.—without offering any clear vision for the future. We have given up the God, yet have retained the ideals. But what grounds values like selflessness, compassion, love of neighbor, and care for the poor without the God who proclaims them? The equality of human beings, for instance, is an idea that comes directly from Christianity. Without the God of Christianity, however, where does that equality come from? What secures it? There's nothing grounding our ideals or giving them substance, and at some level we know this. That is why we live in an age of outrage, where people feel personally attacked when they are asked to justify their beliefs. The truth is, we can't justify what we stand for because we have no idea what we stand on.

The last man lacks the assurance that he's on the right path, the security we felt as children when we believed our fathers could protect us and our God was watching over us. And what follows is a loss of passion, a loss of meaning, a loss of love. We are no longer willing to do anything boldly, vigorously. The last man is this melancholic nobody, slouching through life filled with despair and yet not fully conscious of the root of his despair. In *The Sickness Unto Death*, Kierkegaard says that just as it takes a good doctor to identify a sickness, so too does it takes a good philosopher—a doctor of the soul, a psychologist—to identify the despair at bottom of humanity's common sickness. For Nietzsche, the despair of modern man is driven by the fact that even though we have given up the God who could orient us, we continue to propagate empty values that no longer make sense. Our ideals are like chaff and we sense how little they mean.

David: *I have a patient who comes from a very strong conservative Evangelical background and has gone through a significant deconstruction. She tells me that she feels absolutely lost—that intellectually, she can't repackage the concepts from her upbringing that she's already taken out of the box, so to speak. She still holds many of those values but doesn't know why. They don't make sense to her anymore. As a result, she feels like she doesn't belong anywhere. So, there's this ongoing angst about who she is apart from the profound ideology that gave her tremendous security for a significant period of her life.*

Lyn: *That makes me wonder whether part of the despair comes from the desire to simply find another box—another community or source of meaning—in which to repackage those values. That sort of fruitless nomadic search might contribute to the sense of despair.*

Yes, I think so. Again, to put it in a Freudian context, it's the child who, recognizing the faults in his father, looks for another role model, a replacement father. For me, when I realized my father did not live up to every idealization I had, I found a professor who I thought might be like my intellectual father and guide me into adulthood. And then it turns out he's also human and therefore flawed, so then I found a colleague who I thought might be a mentor. But we do this again and again, and there is despair in recognizing that we don't really have what we thought we had in our idealized fathers—that security, stability, and source of meaning. Once that has been fractured, you keep searching, but you won't find something to replace it. And your searching only propagates the problem.

> Lyn: *It seems like Freud would say the solution is to find a wife or partner—he says to give up the Oedipal and replace neurotic misery with "ordinary unhappiness," which I take to be marriage. I'm half joking of course, but there is this idea of being able to sublimate and substitute in the Freudian model.*

Yes, in my reading of Freud, the best we can do is to learn to live unhappily, without the interruptions of neuroses. But Nietzsche, I think, is far from that. It's true that in some ways, Nietzsche never wants to abandon the tragic nature of existence. Life will always have struggle and suffering and all types of conflict and problems. But he wants to make sense out of that and consider how we can make the best of that. The last man—this slouching toward despair and nihilism—is the worst outcome. Zarathustra proclaims as much to the people in the marketplace, and in response they ask him to teach them how to be the last man. Zarathustra is of course discouraged by that and realizes that he's speaking to the wrong audience—they don't understand him.

In the Prologue to *Zarathustra*, Nietzsche is synthesizing Plato, Heraclitus, Shakespeare, Dante, Homer, and others, which, artistically is very impressive. Historically, Zarathustra, also known as Zoroaster, was an ancient Iranian prophet, and arguably the first philosopher in history. So, it's worth noting that Nietzsche is taking this father figure in philosophy and making him into the new philosopher for the modern world. Now, Zarathustra, at the age of 30, retreats to the mountains, seeking seclusion from the world, and stays there for ten years. And after a decade of solitude, he looks at the sun and has a revelation: what would the sun be if it couldn't shine on me? The sun, overflowing with joy, promise, and life, is giving itself to me. It isn't content with remaining within itself; it needs to give. Having realized this, Zarathustra decides to descend from the mountains in order to give of himself, in emulation of the sun.

As Zarathustra returns to civilization, he comes across three characters, each of whom represents another way (in addition to the last man) to approach the loss of meaning: the hermit, the tightrope walker, and the jester. All three, Nietzsche wants to tell us, are good possible responses. It might seem that Nietzsche means to disparage the religious response of the hermit, but I think he sees that there is much to admire in the hermit's seclusion. So, Zarathustra comes across this hermit who is living in isolation in the woods, and the first thing he notices is that the hermit is very old. And the first thing the hermit notices about Zarathustra is that he's very young: you look like a child, he tells him. The hermit tells Zarathustra that he shouldn't return to human beings, but rather he should remain in the wilderness and worship God. The hermit's response to the loss of God and the loss of meaning is one of denial. Admitting the terrible truth is, for him, unthinkable. Instead he shelters himself from it. The hermit is laughing in the forest, singing hymns of praise, weeping—he's thoroughly human in that way. But he's lost the childlike nature of Zarathustra. When you suppress something so significant, it weighs on you. The hermit has lost his love of his fellow human beings and now views them with contempt. Zarathustra, young and idealistic, wants to give his fellow man the gift of wisdom. But the hermit says that if he's going to give them something, he should make them beg for alms, because that's what they really want anyway. They want to be given something meager, not something extraordinary. The hermit is hanging onto his love for God, but in doing so has developed a profound contempt for human beings.

I think we see the hermit today as well. He is those people who put their heads in the sand when a terrible truth comes along and double down on their own truth claims. But to some extent, I don't think Nietzsche is entirely disparaging of that. It makes sense to respond that way and there may be some value in it. Zarathustra tells the hermit that he's not going to try to give him anything and that he should leave before he takes anything away from him. What he would take away, of course, is the hermit's naïve clinging to the old meaning, the old view of life. Out of charity to the hermit, Zarathustra leaves him behind. And Nietzsche says the two are laughing like schoolboys as he goes, so there is a kind of reciprocity between them.

Continuing on, Zarathustra comes to the marketplace, which is significant for a number of reasons. For instance, the madman in *The Gay Science* also comes down to the marketplace—the place where humans meet to buy and sell goods. It is the setting of civilized life. It is where the creditor and debtor make their deals. It is the city center. And here, Zarathustra ignores the hermit's advice and tries to offer his wisdom. In response, he is laughed at and sneered at, just as the madman was when he announced the death of God. As Zarathustra speaks, a tightrope walker starts walking across a tightrope suspended between two buildings overhead. And Zarathustra says that actually, humans are tightrope walkers—on our way from one thing to something else. We are not a goal or a finished product. Our task has not been accomplished. Part of the oppression of God and morality is that these sources of meaning take human life as fixed and final and treat it as if it has already reached its conclusion. The meaning of life becomes whatever that defined ideal ascribes to it. But for Nietzsche, human beings, are open-ended. We're not a set thing. I experience this all the time—I think of myself as something and my identity calcifies around that, but then my life changes and I realize I'm actually full of possibility. We are open-ended creatures. So, Zarathustra talks about humans as being on the way to something, like bridges to somewhere new.

In the Kaufman translation, this somewhere new is called the "overman." Others translate it as "superman." This is a very important term in Nietzschean context and is often misunderstood. The overman is not some future creature that we, as humanity, are all striving to become—some perfect, futuristic being. Nietzsche is not a transhumanist. He is likely adapting this idea from an essay by Emerson called "The Over Soul." (Emerson, by the way, had a major influence on Nietzsche.) The overman is something we are *always* on our way to becoming. In a previous meeting, we talked about the sovereign individual as someone who sets personal goals and strives and struggles toward those goals. And when the sovereign individual reaches a goal, already in reaching it, he has transcended that goal and is on the way to something new. So, Nietzsche has this idea for humans to always be striving toward something more. The overman is that *always more*—always overcoming limits and trying to do something more.

David: *What I'm getting from reading this, though, is that no one really gets there. There's no faith whatsoever. It seems like he's saying we are moving toward the overman on an evolutionary scale, and that it's accidental in some sense. Then just a few people get there.*

I think that for Nietzsche, none of us are excluded from the possibility of striving toward the overman, but the problem is that so few of us want to strive. So many of us are the last man, are members of the herd. Nietzsche writes that the last man says he's found happiness—"and he blinks." The last man asks, "What is love? What is creation? What is longing? … and he blinks" (Z, "Prologue," §5). It's this completely lackadaisical attitude. Nietzsche thinks it's rare that humans want to struggle, want to overcome, want to see their lives as constantly striving toward something. I might be reading him too democratically, or maybe reading Emerson into him too much, because Nietzsche is still very much an elitist. But my reading is that it's not that anyone is excluded from the possibility, it's just that very few of us want it. We don't desire it.

Lyn: *Does Nietzsche think it's possible to actually achieve this or is the point the struggle?*

The point is the struggle. It's similar to Dostoevsky's *Notes from the Underground* in a lot of ways. We don't actually want to reach the end goal. Dostoevsky uses the example of chess: the whole point of chess is the game. Once the game is over, there's nothing left to be done. The enjoyment is in the thinking and the strategy—in the playing—more so than in the winning. Human existence is like that. Ideally, we are always on our way to the overman. But it's never something accomplished or realized.

Lyn: *It's like T.S. Eliot says—for us, there's only the trying. The rest is none of*
          our concern.

Yes, that's exactly it. Even if we reach some goal, we'd already be on our way to
the next one or we'd be destroying whatever we just accomplished. Those are
the two options. So in the tightrope walker, Zarathustra sees an image of what
he wants us to see ourselves as. But the tightrope is over an abyss, and we're liable
to fall. This is one of the reasons so many of us refuse to strive. And the tightrope
walker in *Zarathustra* does fall. The people in the marketplace look up at the
tightrope walker and all of a sudden, a jester comes out from a door behind him
and starts prodding him and hitting him. The jester is taunting him and threa-
tening to jump over him if he doesn't move along, and through all this, the
tightrope walker is trying very hard to keep his balance. Then the jester does a flip
in the air and lands on the rope in front of the tightrope walker, and the tightrope
walker falls to his death. As he's lying on the ground, maimed and mangled, he
looks up at Zarathustra, says the devil is going to come to take him to hell, and
asks whether Zarathustra will try to stand in his way. Zarathustra responds by
announcing the death of God once more. He tells the tightrope walker not to
worry because there is no afterlife. And the tightrope walker has this stirring
insight in his final moments: if there's no afterlife, no good and evil, no right and
wrong, then we're nothing more than brute animals that have been taught to
perform with the carrot and the stick—our morality amounts to the domesti-
cation of an animal trained by punishments and rewards (Z, "Prologue," §6).
We've seen that, in some ways, Nietzsche agrees with this assessment of social
life. But here Zarathustra rebuts it as slander and offers the dying man some
consolation. He tells him that by making danger his living as a tightrope walker,
he lived vigorously—at least he had the courage to try. He was on his way to the
overman and there is no shame in his dying for that vocation. Zarathustra says
that he will honor his memory by burying his body. The tightrope walker
struggled and triumphed in that struggle, even if it cost him his life.
    The first response to the loss of meaning, that of the hermit, is to bury one's
head in the sand. The second, that of the tightrope walker, is to see the problem,
confront the problem, and fall into the abyss. He reminds us of Hamlet—he
doesn't know what to do and is looking for a way forward, but it's a hard and
dangerous road, and living in the absence of God/the father leaves one liable to fall.

David: *A quick anecdote: My first internship in clinical training was at a very*
          prestigious hospital, and I was anxious to learn from these esteemed psychiatrists
          and analysts. The first case conference I sat in on was a young college student
          who had attempted suicide and was in the ward being treated for massive
          depression. I asked the lead psychiatrist what the precipitant was for the suicide
          attempt, and he said that the student had taken a course in existentialism. I
          asked what the treatment plan was, to which the psychiatrist said with a
          completely straight face: "stop reading that shit."

Right—that's unfortunately the predicament. Camus compares the tightrope walker to the absurd man in *The Myth of Sisyphus*. Someone who lives that way may be liable to commit suicide or descend into madness, but to warn him of those possibilities doesn't prevent him from trying to live out that confrontation. If you stare too much into the abyss, you might fall in. For Nietzsche, and for Zarathustra, that's an honorable thing. There is some value in that, or at least it's not something to look down upon or sneer at. It's worthwhile—so much so that Zarathustra carries the tightrope walker's body and buries it.

The third possible response to the loss of meaning is embodied by the jester. In Thomas More's *Utopia*, in Shakespeare's plays, in *Don Quixote*, and all over the literary tradition, the fool or dunce is the character who tells the truth and gets away with it because everyone views him as a buffoon—someone to laugh at, someone to sneer at, someone to be mocked. In *Lear*, the Fool is the only one who can tell the king he's lost his mind. He's the only one who can speak candidly and not be punished. In *Utopia*, More advises prospective political philosophers that if they're going to give advice to a prince that conflicts with the status quo or the interests of those in power, they ought to do so in jest. You can tell the truth, he says, but it has to be done farcically; otherwise, you'll be endangering yourself and run the risk of being dismissed or condemned. Nietzsche is playing with this literary trope. The fool catches Zarathustra right before he leaves town and tells him that everyone in the town hates him. Zarathustra speaks the truth and they hate him for it. The jester tells him that they were going to kill him until they saw him talking to the dying tightrope walker. That made them think he was something of a fool. "It was your good fortune that you were laughed at," the jester says (Z, "Prologue," §8). For, anyone who wants to shed light on difficult topics and share uncomfortable truths better do so foolishly or else risk becoming an enemy of the mob. Note that the jester follows his own advice. He sees the tightrope walker, representing humanity itself, slowly meandering across the rope, struggling, scared, and looking down into the abyss, and he tells him to speed up and prods him along. But he does so as a clown.

At the end of the "Prologue," Zarathustra reflects on how painful it is that human beings can be knocked to their death by a fool. Yet the fool serves an important purpose. He alone will be listened to, and Nietzsche is often playing the fool. He allows himself to be woefully misunderstood as a mean, nasty, sneering figure. He intentionally presents himself that way. But by all accounts, he was a meek, humble, very polite, mild-mannered man. There's something funny about a small, frail, soft-spoken scholar writing books about "Why I am so Wise" and the superman and blood and torture and the triumph of Napoleon. I think Nietzsche realizes that a good dose of humor, including taking oneself lightly and allowing oneself to be chastised as a fool, is one way to awaken people to the things they are missing. (We shouldn't forget that Silenus—whose terrible wisdom gave rise to the keenest insight in *Birth*—was a kind of drunken fool and truthteller.) So, the fool's approach to meaninglessness is to make of himself a buffoon. The madman carries a lantern during the daylight hours into the marketplace to look for the invisible God. He is met with laughter. There's a reference to Diogenes there, the ancient philosopher who would go into the marketplace with a lantern looking for a human being. For him, no one lives up to the ideal of what it means to be a human being. The madman does the same thing. For him, no value lives up to the idol of what it means to be God.

So, in these three persons we have three possible ways of coping with the horror of the death of God, the loss of orientation in the world. Although I believe Nietzsche thinks that all of them are valuable in some way, none of them accomplish what he's after. At the end of the "Prologue," Zarathustra buries the corpse of the tightrope walker in a tree (of course, this is an allusion to the tree in the Book of Genesis). He falls asleep, and when he wakes up, he realizes that he is not meant to preach to the crowds. He won't find heroes there, he says. Instead, what he must do is find friends. It's not his job to convert people or change the world. He would only be met with opposition from people who want to put their heads in the sand, and laughter from those who will see him as a fool. And if he proclaims the truth too loudly, he'll be chastised and may even harm others—like the tightrope walker or the hermit or this patient of David's who attempted suicide. It's always a possibility that opening someone's eyes can do more harm than good. Rather, Zarathustra's goal will be to find companions— those who possess spirits like him, who can grapple with hard, immoral, unchristian truths. But he doesn't want people to follow him as disciples; he wants to find those who are like-minded in that they are willing to do the hard work for themselves. They are willing to walk the path of life in the absence of meaning. It's a confusing, winding path into the wilderness. And so, Zarathustra ends up walking deep into the wilderness and getting lost looking for companions.

In *Beyond Good and Evil*, and elsewhere as well, Nietzsche writes as though he is addressing his friends. He calls the reader "friend." I think he is calling for other thinkers, philosophers, or anyone who wants to struggle with these ideas to join him in doing so, but in their own way. Zarathustra is very clear that he doesn't want followers. He wants people to carve their own paths into the same uncharted, terrifying wilderness. But it's a very dangerous way to live, because if you lose your way, you might not make it back. This again speaks to his elitism—he's looking for the few who are willing to do this and are strong enough to persevere. And an essential part of that is being able to see the humor in the pain as well. Returning to the preface to *The Birth of Tragedy*, Nietzsche quotes Zarathustra in defining his aims as a writer. He says that what we need is to "learn the art of *this-worldly* comfort" (BT, "Attempt at Self-Criticism," §7). Those who find *this-worldly* comfort are those who don't flee to God, the afterlife, and morality, but seek out comfort in *this* life: "You ought to learn to laugh, my young friends, if you are hell-bent on remaining pessimists. Then perhaps, as laughers, you may some day dispatch all meta-physical comforts to the devil" (§7). And in a very funny turn, he says that

Zarathustra understands this most of all and proceeds to quote him—to quote his own text:

> The crown of laughter, the rose-wreath crown: I crown myself with this crown; I myself pronounced holy my laughter. I did not find anyone else today strong enough for that. … This crown of laughter, the rose-wreath crown: … Laughter I have pronounced holy: you higher men, *learn*—to laugh! (§7)

So, a big part of his project overall is to find people who can do this very difficult thing, but in a light-hearted way—be able to laugh at that which pains you and see the humor in yourself and in the absurdity of life.

David: *Related to this idea of looking for a kind of friendship, in a couple passages I noticed that Nietzsche seems to be a proponent of certain types of marriage as a way of bringing out the best in each other. Even though he prided his singleness, he appears to anticipate some of the more contemporary thought in theology about relational spirituality—the journeying together and the mystical tradition of spiritual friends.*

Nietzsche is a very slippery thinker for this reason. The death of God doesn't necessarily exclude the possibility of gods. Nietzsche wants to bring the transcendent down to human lives, for us to see that within our own lives, we might be capable of embodying a type of divinity. So, yes, there is a resonance there with contemporary theologies, because for Nietzsche, part of being the overman is being transcendent yourself. In a way, he's a very religious thinker, but a religious thinker who wants to live out the absence of God. God's not there. The "big Other" of Lacan that oversees everything doesn't exist. But here is divinity within this life itself—within our friendships, within our relationships, within our humor. And honestly, what's funnier than marriage? Could anything be so idiotic and yet so essential? (Don't tell my wife I said that.) In marriage, we find the transcendent in the immanent, but also the hilarity and absurdity of life thrust before us on a daily basis. So there is something divine in the pain and the turmoil and the humor of the hearth and home.

David: *It almost sounds like Paul Tillich's "God above God" and the type of pantheism he espouses.*

Yes, and Nietzsche is very inspired by ancient Greek religions, pre-Plato—the god of Socrates and the deities and quasi-deities embodied in human form.

Jason: *In reading Nietzsche and reading biographies about him, I'm wondering if he may have had bipolar disorder. I think that has been suggested by others as well. And if that's true, and I think it's clear that at the end of his life he was very out-of-touch with reality, I think it makes some of these ideas even more sympathetic. That is,*

I think Nietzsche may have known personally what it was like to be thought a madman or a fool, and at the same time, to have a sense of grandiosity—that "I'm better than them" and "they're just not up to my speed." I think these ideas are embodied in a manic experience; it's a sublimation of a manic experience.

The fact that he personifies madness in the madman or the fool inoculates him, to some degree, against criticism and skepticism because there is that manic defense: "If you criticize this or don't agree with this, it's just because you're not enlightened enough to understand it." On the other hand, I find it very inspirational. When I read this, it makes me want to be an overman. I want to be manic with him. It sounds very condescending when both these characters—Zarathustra and the madman—just walk away and say I'm not ready for them. It makes me want to say, "but I am ready for you!" I'm ready. Be friends with me, you know?

[**Editor's Note:** *This comment is followed by a round of laughter.*]

In Nietzsche's biography, you're right—it's obvious there's some psychosis there. Of course, he had some horrible physical ailments as well. He had crippling gastrointestinal problems that kept him bedridden for days on end. He had horrible migraines and at times was barely able to move. And then when he'd come out of that, he would be completely manic. He had been in so much pain that all he could do was think about how much pain he was in. So, when he was physically able to write, he would write manically. And in the span of just a few years, he produced all of these books. In genius fashion, he wrote everything he could write before ultimately succumbing to madness and spending the last decade of his life as an invalid in the care of his sister.

There's a famous story of him seeing a horse being beaten, and it so moved him that he ran outside to try to stop the man who was beating it. He flung his arms around the horse's neck and collapsed, and that was the last time anyone saw him in public. He's definitely a bit of a mad figure. (That story is oddly similar to a dream recounted by the protagonist of Dostoevsky's *Crime and Punishment, by the way*.) But he's also inspired by the idea from Plato and the Greeks that madness can be two things: it can be a curse or it can be a gift from the gods. There's a type of madness that comes from above. And if you're filled with that divine madness, you are one of the gifted ones. So in *The Birth of Tragedy*, Nietzsche asks if there is a psychosis or neurosis of health. And he answers yes—and he has it. He might be manic and insane, but that is actually his gift—he can see things that other people can't.

Jason: *In the South we have a saying when someone is crazy, we say that they're touched. And what that meant originally was touched by God—that people who are mad or crazy are touched by God.*

It's the double-play on the word "possessed" too. You can be possessed, as in by demons, or possessed, as in a man possessed is ready to go, ready to do something. The divine and the demonic for Nietzsche, as for Kierkegaard, are not always easy to parse. The madman and the genius are very close to one another.

Jean-Luc: *The artist is the brother of the murderer and the madman, as Thomas Mann says.*

A.M. Pelos: *I'm finding a tension between the idea of abandoning meaning altogether and the idea of having an internal creation of meaning that, while it might be malleable or transient, still grounds certain aspects of your life. Do you think Nietzsche is leaning one way or the other?*

It's an excellent question. In some places, it seems that Nietzsche is suggesting—and Zarathustra evens says this—that the overman should be the meaning of the world. So the question is whether he is setting up a new ideal for us. We know he wants to abandon the old values. But we don't want to have no values at all, so they must be replaced with new values, new ideas. So, on the one hand, we have this idea that you can create meaning. Sartre will take up Nietzsche on this point and say that it's up to each of us to make our own lives meaningful—to create meaning for ourselves. On the other hand, it seems like Nietzsche is giving up on the search for meaning and replacing it with living *à la* Camus. He has this idea of the immanence of things, and to some degree to ask the question of meaning is to be looking either backward toward where your meaning comes from or forward toward when you're going to accomplish something meaningful. It's either behind you or ahead of you. But notions like *amor fati* or the eternal recurrence, these really important ideas for Nietzsche, seem to point us away from meaning and toward living. Stop worrying about meaning and instead live vigorously and fully. Life is fleeting, right?

I don't know which position he settles on, ultimately. But again, Nietzsche is very willing to contradict himself and doesn't see that as a fault. He thinks a broad person can contradict himself. A narrow person is too consistent—it's a restraint. Being broad means being able to think all things or say all things. So, at times he does contradict himself, and on these points in particular.

Well, it's been a pleasure to get together on my birthday and go through these texts. I always enjoy our conversations. And now I'm going to go put a birthday candle in a glass of whiskey and call it a night. Until next time.

*[**Editor's Note:** Another round of laughter follows as the group begins to disperse.]*

Jean-Luc: *Wait, didn't you say something about returning to Nietzsche's relationship with his father—*

*[**Editor's Note:** The recording ends here.]*

5 Fifth Meeting 05/26/2022

Our Virtue: An Honest Look at Suffering and Joy

Beyond Good and Evil is perhaps Nietzsche's most mature and philosophically impressive work. I think it's also his most difficult to read because, as I realized while prepping for tonight, there is no systematic way to approach it. Nietzsche's texts tend to be a bit anarchic—he writes like a modernist poet—but at least in *Birth* and *Genealogy,* there are clear progressions of thought running through. *Beyond Good and Evil*, on the other hand, consists of ideas that flash like lightning—they might be related to one another or contradict one another, and they take us in new and surprising directions. This may be due in part to how Nietzsche wrote this work—he would write in small bursts, going for walks and then coming home to write frantically whatever was on his mind—but I think it also speaks deeply to Nietzsche's philosophy and his way of thinking: ideas ought to be interesting, provocative, challenging, not necessarily true. The value of truth, his style suggests, is something we ought to question. Why not prefer a charming lie—a work of art—over a sterile logical proof?

He also writes in this text about how understanding great literary or philosophical thinkers means not only grappling with their ideas, but also appreciating their style, their tempo, their form—*how* they write. *Beyond Good and Evil* is a fast-paced work. You fly through it as you read. And that element is itself significant to understanding what Nietzsche means to accomplish. He's not trying to lay out a philosophical system. The subtitle, "Prelude to a Philosophy of the Future," indicates as much. This is merely a beginning, an opening, a condition of possibility for something to arise. As such, it is meant to throw ideas scattershot at the reader which may initiate in him an impetus to move forward and begin philosophizing anew. I think Freud, for instance, takes up certain themes from this text and runs with them in exactly the sense that Nietzsche is calling future thinkers to do. Camus does so as well, but in very different directions. As do Heidegger and Sartre, though there are ways in which they distort some of Nietzsche's central insights. Anyway, that's my preface to tonight's meeting. I'll do my best to offer some sort of structure going forward, at least to how we might

DOI: 10.4324/9781003348795-5

think about some of the major threads that run through this work, but I make no promises. My job is merely to provoke and perhaps to entertain.

❖

At the beginning of §227, which is located in Part 7, "Our Virtues," Nietzsche posits: "Honesty, supposing that this is our virtue from which we cannot get away, we free spirits—well, let us work on it with all our malice and love and not weary of 'perfecting' ourselves in *our* virtue, the only one left us." Of course, honesty has long been considered a virtue. But in Nietzsche's hands, it takes on new meanings. To understand why, we must begin by contrasting it with a concept it is typically related to—truth. But truth and honesty need not go together. One must only consider the myriad deceptions employed by philosophers—those self-proclaimed lovers of truth—to grasp as much. Nietzsche writes:

> What provokes one to look at all philosophers half suspiciously, half mockingly, is not that one discovers again and again how innocent they are … but that they are not honest enough in their work, although they all make a lot of virtuous noise when the problem of truthfulness is touched even remotely. They all pose as if they had discovered and reached their real opinions through the self-development of a cold, pure, divinely unconcerned dialectic (as opposed to the mystics of every rank, who are more honest and doltish—and talk of "inspiration"); while at bottom it is … most often a desire of the heart that has been filtered and made abstract that they defend with reasons they have sought after the fact. (BGE, 1, §5)

Truth, Nietzsche tells us, is the name we often use to baptize our prejudices. We claim truth as our mantle only to conceal dishonest motives. But the "free spirit," that friend of Zarathustra's who, as I mentioned last seminar, is not a disciple but a sovereign willing to risk himself and beclown himself for the sake of his values, who keeps his word not out of fear but integrity, self-reliance, and self-respect—he knows better. He's too honest to insist that truth is on his side. He knows that he does not know what truth is.

Beyond Good and Evil opens with the memorable question: "Supposing truth is a woman—what then?" (BGE, "Preface"). Assuming an understanding of sexual difference reminiscent of Lacan's, Nietzsche asks us to consider whether truth is—as it has traditionally been thought to be—clear, definable, stable, rational, abstract; or whether, in truth, it is actually something enigmatic, evasive, other, fluid, impossible to nail down, impossible to grasp and hold onto. Unlike philosophers such as Plato with his unchangeable forms, Aristotle with his logic, Descartes with his clear and distinct ideas, Hegel with his system, and old Kant with his categories,

Nietzsche suggests that we ought to move away from the hyper-logical, hyper-masculine paradigm that has dominated western thought. He recasts truth as something fundamentally unknowable. In this way, he echoes the greatest psychological insight from Socrates—wisdom is knowing that one knows not. Philosophers, he says, tend to be dishonest about truth. In treating their ideas as if they are divinely inspired (Descartes literally says as much in his third mediation) and treating themselves as if they have uncovered some sort of firm grounding upon which their philosophies are based, they lie about truth, about their relation to it, and, most importantly, about themselves. An honest philosopher, for Nietzsche, begins by recognizing that truth is evasive—it masks itself and presents itself at times in one way and at times in another. Truth is not something we can claim as our own. And the more we insist upon it, the further we are from it.

To illustrate this idea, I'll give what might be a useful example. When my wife and I argue, I'm generally insisting that I know the truth of the situation—that *this* is what happened, *this* is what we're fighting about, and *this* is how we fix it. I have a quintessentially masculine approach and, in so far as I assert my authority with regards to the truth, I am thoroughly dishonest and woefully stupid. The truth is, the situation is always more complex than I am willing to admit and my truth is only ever that—*my* truth, as seen from my perspective. To deny or ignore this fact is to lie, both to others and myself. Similarly, Nietzsche claims that philosophers are often dishonest in the way they make their claims and insist upon the veracity of their arguments. If, however, one wants honesty to be one's characteristic virtue, one must begin by letting go of his dedication to truth at all costs. One must be too honest for that.

Honesty, Nietzsche claims, means being willing to admit that at times, deception and lies are fundamental parts of life. Untruth is as necessary for human existence as truth. This is evident in even the most mundane aspects of civilized society, such as the rules of the road. As we noted in our first seminar, driving on the right side of the road is an artificial construction made up by human beings in order to help us—by means of an untruth—to make our way through the world. There is no necessity behind it. There's nothing compelling us to abide by it. But of course, by pretending it is necessary, it becomes a very valuable and useful tool—it keeps us safe and allows us to coexist with one another. Think of the chaos that would ensue if we ceased believing in such lies. In *Genealogy*, Nietzsche points out that even our highest ideals are manmade untruths. Where is *justice* in nature? Where is *equality*? Where *freedom*? Such values are invented. It speaks to the artistry of human beings that we can hold them as immutable laws. In all honesty, dishonesty, appearance, artifice, masks—these are fundamental aspects of human experience, and Nietzsche wants us to be adult enough to admit it.

But honesty means more than this. Not only does Nietzsche highlight the problem of human constructs, but as we have said, he also draws our attention to the fact that each of us approaches the world from his own individual perspective and none of us can fully remove himself from it. There is no objective knowledge or objective standard by which to judge things (or if there is, we don't have access to it). This idea relates somewhat to our last discussion: giving up the God that provides us with meaning and stability is like giving up the illusion of objective truth that provides us with a sense of certainty in life. Even something like a scientific approach, say, a neurological approach to understanding the human psyche, is just another perspective from which to view things. Is it truer than other perspectives? Without question, in that it can account for more of life, explain more of existence. But is it the truth itself? No good scientist would claim that.

Of course, we are free to adopt whichever perspective or perspectives help us to make our way through the world. But for Nietzsche, if we are going to commit ourselves to the kind of honesty that acknowledges the limits of human understanding, we must give up the illusory belief in an objectivity that no human being could ever possess. We must think psychologically rather than logically, interrogating life as we encounter it rather than living on abstractions. Nietzsche claims that the time has come to return psychology to its proper place as "queen of the sciences" (BGE, 1, §23). That is, we need to bring our questions, our concerns, and our focus back down to the level of human beings and human relations. We need to focus on understanding ourselves first and foremost—our values and the value of those values, for instance. While philosophers have traditionally written about the nature of God, the nature of being, and the origins and structure of the cosmos, getting lost in metaphysical abstractions, what is needed most is a return to *the real*, to the human subject and life as it presents itself.

In calling for philosophy to return to that which is most fundamental—the human psyche, what shapes it, and how it can flourish—Nietzsche suggests that we don't simply need "new philosophers," but new psychologists as well (BGE, 1, §23). Perhaps unsurprisingly, he wants to move beyond the type of moral psychology that concerns itself with right and wrong, good and evil, in human behavior. Rather, he insists that we should strive to become more honest psychologists, which means letting go of our own moral prejudices. We saw the problems Nietzsche identifies in the moral worldview when we read *Genealogy*. The moral perspective is just that—a perspective—and we fall into the same trap every time we adopt a single perspective as gospel truth. What's more, moral thinking propagates a view of how life ought to be. This is a struggle all human beings face, an implicit belief in objective moral standards. We recognize it when we hear ourselves saying things like "I *should* have done this," "she *should* be more like that," "you *oughtn't* feel that way," "there's something wrong with me," etc. We compare ourselves to others and make all sorts of subtle moral claims that assume there is some true moral standard to which behavior should adhere. If we accept these claims as true, however—that someone ought to be different, for example—then we are prevented from seeing other people, ourselves, and the world as they really are. To impose our "oughts" and "shoulds" onto the world is to impose a fictional framework onto reality and claim it as truth itself.

Notice, however, that Nietzsche is a very slippery thinker. We were just saying that lies are necessary and valuable; fictions are very important for human life. Morality is such a fiction and it has its value, so long as we're honest enough to admit that it's a fiction—that it doesn't represent the world as it is. We have to separate the world as it is from the world as we would like it to be. We tend to assume that there is something degenerate with the world because it doesn't conform to our standards. This, Nietzsche says, is the source of all sorts of psychoses and other maladies that plague human beings. The world as it is may be full of violence, meanness, and chaos, but it's also full of excessive joy and overflowing creativity. The world doesn't take into account our categories of good and evil. This is obvious if we look at nature. My children like to watch documentaries about animals and they sometimes ask me to join them. What immediately strikes you as you watch is that the very same animal can, at one moment, content itself with ripping its neighbor limb from limb and, at the next, show great love and care for its offspring. There's no discordance within the animal world; the animal sees no problem with that duality. Indeed, there is no duality. What we do when we observe this apparent contradiction is impose our ideas of good and evil upon a world that presents no such binaries. My son will say that he hopes the lion doesn't catch the gazelle. He's mapping his moral framework onto the situation, whereas life simply is what it is. Nietzsche notes that we falsify the world by pretending that it should be other than it is.

But it's not just the world that we misrepresent and malign with our slanderous truth claims. Objective moral standards push conformity and a spurious necessity on human beings, demanding that we act like and be like that which we are not. We reduce ourselves and one another to the level of what Nietzsche calls the "herd animal." He uses this term again and again as a reproach and reminder that human beings are meant for more than the trivial pleasures and stultifying labor to which society consigns them. It's a term with a long philosophical history that dates back to Plato's political writings (the *Statesman*, for instance, and the *Laws*). Plato argues that the goal of politics is to impose a regime on human behavior in order to domesticate us and make us as docile as herd animals. There's no denying that socialization aims at conformity, making us more orderly, more civilized, more understandable, less dangerous. (Emerson and Thoreau never tire of reminding us of this point.) Nietzsche, of course, finds this repugnant. He sees it as a profound reduction of human beings and human potential. He has a deep admiration for what people are capable of accomplishing. On the one hand, we're capable of real wickedness, extreme brutality, savagery, barbarism; on the other hand, we're capable of awe-inspiring greatness and aspiring to unimaginable intellectual, performative, and artistic heights. These extremes—the good and the evil—he believes are closely tied to one another. And if that's the case, then when we use morality and politics and socialization to reduce wickedness, we also reduce human potential and negate our capacity for greatness, for accomplishing wonderous things.

Although Nietzsche believes that there are only a few great individuals who can rise above the herd mentality, I think he also finds it problematic that the rest of us are reduced to living like swine. In other words, it's not merely an issue that the potentially great are being held back; it's also an issue that all humans are trapped in systems that reduce us and make us less than what we otherwise could be. For instance, he says perhaps the rule of human existence is not mediocrity with the exception of a few great geniuses; perhaps the rule is great genius, except that chance and fate and other purblind doomsters get in the way of countless would-be geniuses and destroy what might have been. Perhaps genius is rare only because countless factors can stand in the way of one's becoming a great genius. It could be that greatness is distributed more broadly than is apparent. In any event, these impediments that come with morality are calcified when we take morality to be true and are dishonest about the fact that it's only one perspective with which to view the world.

What, then, is really at the bottom of human existence? What are we deep down? What does it mean to be thinking beings, psyches incarnated in the world? For Nietzsche, the essence of all life, not just human life, is what he calls "will to power." Now, will to power is a difficult concept to unpack because Nietzsche says a lot of contradictory things about it, but I'll do my best to articulate what I think he means. Will to power is the drive that compels us forward. It is the drive to overcome resistances, the drive toward excess and overflowing greatness. It is the thing that pushes us to be better and to exert our wills upon the world. For Nietzsche, all life can be understood in terms of the conflicts between individual instantiations of will to power. All life is this insatiable thrust forward. But there is, perhaps, a duality to this drive, just as in Freudian drive theory—the will to power seeks both to dominate and to give of itself, to assert itself and to expend itself. This is very much in line with Freud's notions of Eros and the death drive that he discusses in *Beyond the Pleasure Principle* and *Civilization and Its Discontents*. Like Freud, Nietzsche also says that physiologists should be hesitant to assert that the survival instinct is the fundamental characteristic of life. Life, he insists, is better understood as the desire to discharge one's power, the need to release tension and express one's dominance and excess. We see this in social situations and in sexual situations, but also in the creation of something new and in the testing and pushing of oneself to extreme limits.

An example: the other night, my son got hit by a ball at his tee-ball game and he was visibly upset. His anger welled up and he needed to discharge his will to power. He was next up at bat, so I put the ball on the tee and told him to take all his anger and direct it at the ball. He crushed it. His drives and emotions and psychical energy crystalized and he was able to channel it in the swing of his bat. Will to power is this need to expel life's energy, to thrust it outward. Of course, as we saw in *Genealogy*, the outward channels can get dammed up and the reserves can reverse course and flow in on the self. This is the cause of bad conscience. But it is will to power all the same. It is the need to express one's inner chaos, the need for discharge. And one can discharge creatively or with cruelty—and perhaps always with a bit of both.

❖

In §36 and 37, Nietzsche lays out a profound, provocative expression of the will to power and then, in typical Nietzschean fashion, puts on a character's voice and questions what he has just said. If all of life is will to power, "Doesn't this mean, to speak with the vulgar: God is refuted, but the devil is not?" In response to this, he simply answers "On the contrary, my friends" and then moves on. What caught my attention here is that he is giving voice to this notion of the imminence of divine power that is constantly thrusting itself through all of life, always seeking its own discharge in creativity and destruction. It's similar to his notion of the Dionysian in *The Birth of Tragedy*—this life force that operates in the world, that each of us is in some mystical sense an individual instantiation of, that seeks to create and destroy and enjoys itself in doing so. Will to power is its own enjoyment of this burst of life energy that will break things apart and put them back together in new ways only to break them apart again.

What does all this mean for the individual and for human psychology? One thing it suggests is that an essential part of who we are is this need to create and destroy, this need to overcome and compete and test ourselves against one another. Recall that we said morality tends to instill in people the idea that there's something wrong with them for having these impulses—that the drives to compete and dominate are problematic. And recall that Nietzsche says an honest psychologist, someone who thinks deeply about human existence, will say that this will to power is actually all we are at bottom. His new philosophers, then, instead of trying to reduce the will to power and reduce people to herd animals, will try to find ways to intensify it and provoke its outward discharge. Of course, this is a dangerous thing because these drives also bring out some of the worst aspects of humanity. But those worst aspects are a part of us too and, as Freud shows, repressing them does nothing to eliminate them. What Nietzsche wants are philosophers and psychologists who can get us to acknowledge and reflect upon these inner truths (perspectival as they might be), and work to exercise them creatively, discharging them in the service of a furthering of human life.

To that end, he wants to rebuff the utilitarian assumption that grounds modern democratic ideals that suffering ought to be treated and reduced at all costs. Contrary to this perspective, Nietzsche's new philosophers will say they want their suffering to increase because they recognize that every great human accomplishment in history is born of suffering. Suffering can be a catalyst; it can inspire you toward remarkable things. If I asked you what defines your life, what are the experiences or events without which you would not be you, chances are you would list some painful and trying challenges you have had to endure. Living through such things, persevering and overcoming in the face of such obstacles, marks you. For better or for worse, it makes you who you are. When I think about what defines me, of course, I think about my marriage. But my marriage entails a lot of suffering. I think about my children, but my children bring me an enormous amount of grief. There are a lot of good things too, but all of the best things in my life have also been the most difficult and most trying.

I think Nietzsche is very perceptive on this point. If you look at where we are socially, able to treat psychological suffering with pharmaceuticals and living in the most prosperous epoch in human history, we seem to be rather unjustified in our discontent. This observation was perhaps more apt pre-pandemic, but we haven't had any major wars in this part of the world in a long time, and technological advances have made us the most comfortable civilization in history. Yet we're all terribly unhappy. We see peace and prosperity and we're committing suicide at staggering rates and drinking ourselves to death and overdosing on drugs. What we see is profound psychological suffering, profound feelings of despair, in the most stable societies. When Putin first invaded Ukraine, a friend asked me whether I thought Americans would show as much resilience as the Ukrainians have. I don't know the answer to that, but there is something about comfort, stability, and success that lends itself to a diminution, a slacking of our capacities to strive and overcome.

Again, for Nietzsche, the philosopher of the future will take life as it is with all its suffering and, rather than try to escape it, will embrace suffering as a potential catalyst. Such an honest thinker, capable of admitting the value of will to power, will see the necessity of offering new values by which human beings can live. He will become a creator of values, the bearer of new and noble ideals. Nietzsche wants to inspire us to look deeply at life and all its problems and to do so honestly. From there, we can become creative and inventive and yield new directions for humanity. He says that there needs to be something inventive in the practice of psychology—something that charts new paths of understanding. Psychology, as another perspective on life, necessarily entails human creativity. For example, when my psychoanalyst asks me questions, what he asks and what he doesn't ask and how he interprets what I tell him and the interpretations he inspires in me all entail creativity on his part. He inspires new perceptions and directions for my life and journeys with me as I live them into existence.

Ultimately, the goal for Nietzsche is to move beyond the social constraints that reduce us to the level of herd animals and inspire us to reach for the heights of human potentiality. What constitutes such heights? Nietzsche offers a hint. Elsewhere, he calls the idea the eternal recurrence of the same and describes as follows:

> What, if some day or night a demon were to steal after you into your loneliest loneliness and say to you: "This life as you now live it and have lived it, you will have to live once more and innumerable times more; and there will be nothing new in it, but every pain and every joy and every thought and sigh and everything unutterably small or great in your life will have to return to you, all in the same succession and sequence—even this spider and this moonlight between the trees, and even this moment and I myself. The eternal hourglass of existence is turned upside down again and again, and you with it, speck of dust!"
>
> Would you not throw yourself down and gnash your teeth and curse the demon who spoke thus? Or have you once experienced a tremendous moment when you would have answered him: "You are a god and never have I heard anything more divine." (GS, 4, §341)

Here in *Beyond Good and Evil*, he asks whether there is anyone capable of saying "*da capo*," "from the beginning," again and again forever (BGE, 3, §56). For Nietzsche, only those who see themselves and the world honestly and have found something to say "Yes" to—something of value that makes life worth living—will be able to say *da capo*. You have to truly and authentically love life and be grateful for life *as it is* in order to agree to bear this tremendous weight. And this is precisely the ideal toward which Nietzsche wants us to aspire.

To follow the thought experiment, consider how much about you would change if you were able to go back and prevent the worst things you have experienced—all the pains and traumas you've suffered—from ever happening. You would no longer be yourself and your life would no longer be aiming at whatever it is aiming at presently. The goal for each of us, then, is to build a life such that we wouldn't change anything about the past, because to do so would mean changing who we are and who we aspire to be. To love oneself and one's life so deeply that one feels gratitude for all he has had to bear is, for Nietzsche, man's crowning achievement. And this is what he sees as being possible for his new philosophers: By looking deeply and honestly at themselves and creating new ways forward, they will not want to deny anything that was or is, precisely because everything has become essential, a necessary part of the journey of self-overcoming.

Jason: Eternal recurrence sounds to me a lot like amor fati. *Are they the same thing or are they overlapping?*

I think the two are fundamentally intertwined. This, to me, is the central idea in Nietzsche. If you want to try to sum up the positive aspects of his philosophy and not simply focus on his diagnoses and critiques, then I think that his idea of the good life is based on loving your fate—so much so that you would live your life again and again forever if you could.

Jason: *Does he intend for it to be prescriptive as well? That is, does he mean that we should proceed in living our lives as if we will have to live them over and over again, and therefore we make intentional choices based on that? Does it provide a kind of, dare I say, moral guide for how to live?*

Well, Nietzsche is aware of and hints at the fact that by demolishing certain moralities, he has to replace them with something else. I think he thinks we can't live without some moral notion, some guiding principle, and that we're fundamentally moral, or valuing, creatures. So, I do think it's a moral prescription of sorts, though certainly different than any of the moralities he critiques. I think he recognizes that there's so much beyond our control, but what we can control is our being open to life as it presents itself and being grateful for that. We can always keep pushing forward and trying to overcome, regardless of what gets thrown at us. If you're able to constantly aspire toward something and make something out of the misery and viciousness of life, then I think Nietzsche would say you're on the right track.

David: *The idea of challenging our morality without outgrowing it is making me think of Bonhoeffer, who during the Second World War left a cushy job and abandoned his pacifist philosophy to join an assassination attempt in Germany. He really gave up on his morality in favor of a completely different one because he felt called to do something of great importance. It's an interesting example of not only getting beyond the herd mentality of the rest of the church in Germany at the time, but also challenging his own deeply held morality and theology in order to do something for which he ultimately paid quite dearly.*

At the end of *The Antichrist*, which is one of Nietzsche's final works, he claims that his whole aspiration is to constantly revaluate all values. In other words, every time you've determined for yourself a system of values to live by and goals to strive toward, be ready to completely unsettle them and question them and dispose of them. In one of his aphorisms, Nietzsche says that anyone who achieves his goal *eo ipso* transcends it. The moment you've accomplished what you were working toward, you've transcended it and moved on to something new. So, you need a further goal to work toward, and that could completely undermine your previous worldview. Life itself is characterized by change, and so the life of the mind should be equally characterized by change: Never have a fixed idea. Never think you're certain of something. Never hold onto something as an absolute truth. There's always reinterpreting to be done and, in a sense, that is the whole process of being alive for Nietzsche.

Lyn: *I'm curious as to what your personal opinion is of Nietzsche's philosophy. What is most meaningful to you, and how are you in conversation with him in your own work?*

I very much like philosophers who tear down other philosophies and I think Nietzsche is a great sword and scalpel for excising problematic ideas. He is at his worst, though, when he is most serious. I get a sense at times that he's really railing as hard as he can as this lone voice shouting in the wilderness. At times, he seems to me to be full of the resentment he so keenly identifies in others. He's at his best, I think, when he's being playful and funny in his writing. This is one of the things that I admired about him in the first place and have come to appreciate even more after rereading him and interpreting him anew. The greatest philosophers are very funny. They're funny because they recognize that with all the absurdity of human life, you can only do so much analyzing and diagnosing before you just have to laugh. But when he's too cynical and resentful, he can be difficult to read. Then when he's witty and clearly having fun and dancing in the way he claims a great thinker can dance, he's an absolute joy to read. I think with Nietzsche, more than with any other philosopher, you can really sense different moods in different passages—as if his works provoke you to identify the feelings you experience when you're reading him. He's unique in that way. You can't understand his ideas unless you look at what they are doing to you, what they are making you feel.

Lyn: *Do you think that at times he takes on a persecutory position? There are times it seems that he feels so bitter and it seems personal and painful in some ways.*

In one of his aphorisms, he says that one should take care when wrestling with monsters not to become a monster. So, I think he's aware that, as he takes on these challenging world-historic thoughts and systems, feelings of persecution and alienation might come up for him. He talks a lot about solitude and being misunderstood, and how the most profound thinkers are always misunderstood. And there are times when it's clear that he views himself as a great thinker who doesn't have a community of equals around him; there's definitely misery and pain in that.

Mary: *On the one hand, his writing feels very personal and, as a reader, grappling with his ideas is a deeply introspective and individual process. But on the other hand, you get the sense that he is speaking to a collective audience that amounts to all of humanity. And I'm wondering, who does he think his audience is?*

It's an interesting question. I've been reading a biography of Nietzsche written by Lou Salomé, who was a friend of his and to whom he proposed twice. She rejected him twice, which may account for some of the animus we were just saying we see in his work. Of course, she knew him and read all his writing and, interestingly, she says that Nietzsche claimed to be writing just for himself. *Mihi ipsi scripsi* was a motto of his—I write myself for myself.

Writing is, of course, a process of self-discovery, a means of inventing and understanding oneself on the page. But I think anyone who claims not to have a reader in mind is being dishonest. Nietzsche clearly has a vision. He's writing a prelude to the future of philosophy—to all future philosophers who will read him. He clearly had a pretty grandiose view of himself. In his autobiography, for instance, he calls himself "a destiny." He has that sense of grandeur, yet I think he also feels the pang of being misunderstood and marginalized because he is at odds with his contemporaries. Kierkegaard can come across in the same way. But it makes you wonder, if they had someone else to share their ideas with, would they have had the same bite and been as perceptive? Being isolated can help you mull the depths, but it can also turn you a bit venomous and acidic.

David: *So much of his writing is exhilarating to read, but part of it is so sad that it's a struggle to read. I wonder whether his style played a role in preventing him from having any serious intimacy or significant relationships. At the same time, I think there's so much potential in his work to be applied to relationships. Some of what he writes about marriage is incredible—there's so much intersubjectivity that resonates with what I see in the room with clients. Yet something about his style, as with Kierkegaard, blocks him from real connection. They both end up sort of miserable and alone.*

Absolutely. Nietzsche has this idea, which I think is really valuable, that you should only challenge ideas you find worthwhile. To challenge someone's views is actually to compliment him because his ideas are good enough for you to challenge. There's something wonderful about that. Yet Nietzsche completely destroyed his relationship with Wagner, who had been a good friend of his. He eviscerated him in his writings and it ruined their relationship. So, even though he admires Wagner as one of the great geniuses of his time, he sacrifices his relationship with a friend for the sake of an idea. He does the same when he's criticizing the "English psychologists" in *Genealogy*, some of whom are his friends. He doesn't just criticize them, he tarnishes them. When he writes about the value of friendship, it does make you wonder why he might not have seen himself as being capable of having one.

Jason: *Like David, I find myself for the most part very inspired and charmed when reading Nietzsche, but at the same time, there can be a condescension that really turns me off. Sometimes I feel he is ambivalent about people and antisocial. In one of his letters, he says, "I am dynamite." Of course, dynamite can blow things up and be destructive in a positive way, but it can also be used as a weapon. That seems to describe him well, I think.*

In *The Gay Science*, there is a section where he's talking to some unknown person and says that the two of them make such a good pair and their friendship seems destined in the stars, but on earth, it cannot be. We'll be enemies on earth and friends in the stars. You get the sense that that's how he viewed a lot of his relationships. Something gets in the way. And he definitely has an ambivalence toward his fellow human beings, even his readers. At times his texts almost say: "Who are you to read and interpret me?" But then—what great genius hasn't felt that fear, that pain at being misunderstood?

David: *I found myself fantasizing about what it would be like to sit in a room with him, and I don't think it would be a particularly pleasant experience. He reminds me of some of my most difficult patients. No matter what I try to interpret or whatever level of empathetic attunement I attempt, they'll say, no—that's not it. That's how he sometimes comes across to me.*

I think he probably felt like he was always the smartest person in the room, and frankly, he probably was. And that would explain some of his difficulty in relating to others, because when you think so deeply about things, you can become nauseated by small talk and the mundane everyday conversations that most people have. I don't think a tenth as deeply as Nietzsche, and I feel this way all the time. I like coaching my kids' tee-ball because it means I don't have to talk to the other parents. I can just be with the kids and enjoy that dynamic. For Nietzsche, that's probably intensified a hundredfold.

Jean-Luc: *And yet, Nietzsche does create friends for himself. Zarathustra, for instance. And the reader whom he always refers to as his friend. It's as if, looking deeply into the world and finding it unsatisfying, he decides to create it anew and populate it with people more to his liking. His will to power does something creative with his self-destructive impulse. He offers new ideals and creates values and even characters who embody them.*

Yes, that's a very Nietzschean insight. And perhaps an excellent note to close on. Thank you for offering it, my friend.

Appendix
Two Eulogies

06/24/2021

Anthony,

The other day your sister asked me what color your hair is—brown like Dominic's or blonde like Jonny's? I told her I don't know. I've been thinking a lot over the past week about all the things I don't know about you. What do you look like? What does your voice sound like? How does it feel to hold you in my arms? I've wondered if you're loud and wild like your brother Jonathan. Or clumsy like Dom. Or sassy like Maria. I've wondered what your first word would have been. Where you would have taken your first steps. How many times you would have tumbled down the stairs like Jonny, taking years off my life in the process. I've wondered what it would have been like to have you sitting in the kitchen while your siblings ran past or sleeping in a cradle next to our bed. I've wondered if my father would have been proven right, that it's a terrible idea to get a puppy three months before you have a new baby, or if you would have loved the dog more than any of us. I've thought about you playing on the beach with Nana and riding on Papa's lawnmower. Sitting on the dock with your Uncle Sean in Maine and chasing Marty around the yard. Opening packages from Auntie Darlene and getting ghostbuster toys from my brother who secretly wants them for himself. I've wondered what song I would have sung to get you to fall asleep and what book would have been your favorite and what things I would have whispered in your ear that nobody would have known but you. I've thought of you sleeping on my shoulder at the back of the church after you've been too loud and of what a good excuse you would have been to take a walk to the back of the church when I'm restless in Mass and want to step out. I've thought about how hard it would have been to raise four kids and how much easier it would have been to raise four kids than to deal with any of this.

I've been thinking about all the things I don't know about you and I've realized that none of them matter because none of them are real. So here, instead, are the things I do know about you. The only things that are real. I know that your name is Anthony Joseph and that you are my son. I know that I love you and that I will never stop missing you. I know that nothing will take this pain from me because I love you and because you are my son. I know that your mother loves you and your brothers love you and your sister loves you and none of them will forget you. I know that it's an honor to be your father and that I will never stop missing you and that I love you, my son. I love you little boy. Goodbye.

02/24/2022

Victoria,

When your brother Anthony died, I thought I would never be happy again. I thought—that's it for me. I'll feel moments of pleasure. I'll enjoy listening to Dom play the piano. I'll laugh when Jonny gets up from the table and dances around the kitchen. I'll feel grateful to have Maria laying on my chest when I'm reading to her at night. I may even find a few brief moments of joy when I let Joey out of his crate and he wags his tail and tries to pull off my socks so he can eat them. But I'll never be happy. Not like I was before. Not like I wanted to be. Losing your brother was too monstrous. I knew I would never get past it. His death would hang over everything. Nothing could set that right.

I woke up one morning around Christmastime and your mother was looking at me. She said, "Are you awake?"—which was a ridiculous thing to say since she was looking me in the eyes. Then she said, "I have some news. I'm pregnant" and all of the sudden, in that moment, I was happy. Happy like I'd never been before. Happy like I never imagined I could be again. Happy without losing one ounce of sadness or pain over losing your brother, but still, impossibly, so filled with love and hope that I realized nothing could take my happiness away.

You only existed in this world for 12 short weeks. Like your brothers and sister before you, you did nothing but make me worry and fear and dread the possibility of having to live through a day like today. Well—now my fears have been realized. You, like Anthony, are gone. But with your life, you did something for me that no one could do. You showed me that it is possible to live through the worst pain and still be happy. Not in spite of that pain, but because of it. Anthony's death was crushing to me because I love him so much. And I see now, as I think about you, my sweet little girl, that that love is my happiness. I will never forget what it was to see your tiny heartbeat. I will never forget that for a short while, your heart beat and my heart beat at the same time, in the same way, filled with the same life. I will never forget how you lived inside your mother, how she cared for you with the entirety of her being, how she gave her body to your body and nourished you with herself. I will never forget how excited your brothers and sister were when we told them you existed, their joy at knowing that you were their sister, their love for you, the love they still give voice to every day. And I will never forget the hope you have given me, the hope that happiness is real and that it is mine every time I think of how much I love you.

You are my daughter, Victoria Rae. You will always be my daughter. And I am forever grateful to you. I love you little girl. Goodbye.

Index

Alexander the Great 22
Apollonian 2, 8–10, 12, 14, 28
Aristotle 3, 56
Athens 7, 33
Augustine 40
Author iii, v, xv–xvii, 1–70

chaos 10–12, 14, 27, 57, 59, 61
character x–xii, xviii, 14, 35, 40, 54, 67
Christendom 17
Christianity 20, 40, 45
civilization 13, 17–19, 41, 43, 46, 62;
        human 22, 30
collective life 30–31
community 12, 23, 27, 30, 65; human 30
conscience: bad 33–37, 43, 61; free 37;
        guilty 34; liberated 37
cruelty 31–35, 37, 61
culture 18, 22, 36, 39–40; American 44

Dante 46
Davis, Miles, *Kind of Blue* 26
Dionysian 2–3, 8–12, 14, 39, 61
Dionysius 3
Dostoevsky 24, 48, 53

equality 15, 17, 45, 57

Feast of Fools 9
freedom 9–10, 37, 57
Freud, Sigmund 2, 8, 13, 17, 19, 34, 36,
        39, 42, 44–46, 55, 60–61; *Beyond
        the Pleasure Principle* 8, 60; *The
        Ego and the Id* 12; *Totem and
        Taboo* 30, 41, 43

God 3–4, 6, 34, 42–45, 47, 49, 51–53, 58,
        61, 63

good and evil 18–19, 35, 49, 58–59
Gospel of Matthew 16
Greeks 4–5, 7, 9, 11, 53

Heraclitus 46
Homer 46
honesty 56–58
human animal 18, 32
human beings 3, 5, 15–20, 26, 29–31, 37,
        39, 41–45, 47, 50–51, 57–59,
        62, 67
human creativity 62
human psychology 33, 61
humility 17, 19, 20
humor 33, 35, 39, 41, 50–52

information 22

Jordon, Michael 19
Judaism 20
justice 22, 57

Kierkegaard 54, 66; *The Sickness Unto
        Death* 45
knowledge 9, 11, 16, 22, 44; men of 15,
        18; objective 58; traumatic 3;
        tree of 19

languages 22, 32, 36
libido 38–39

masculine 39, 57
meanness 4, 36, 59
memory 29–32, 36–37, 39, 49
misery 3, 25, 64–65
Mitis (King) 3
modesty 17
morality 5–6, 9, 12, 17, 20, 26–27, 37–38,

41, 47, 49, 51, 59–61; aristocratic
18; herd 15; normative 35; slave
15, 18–19, 23
More, Thomas, *Utopia* 50

Napoleon 21, 50
National Socialist movement 20
Nietzsche, Friedrich: "Attempt at Self-
Criticism" 5; bad conscience 33;
Beyond Good and Evil 2, 39, 51,
55–56, 63; *The Birth of Tragedy*
2–3, 5, 7–10, 21, 23, 36, 51, 53;
The Brothers Karamazov 24;
Civilization and Its Discontents 13,
60; *The Gay Science* 41, 44;
Genealogy is *Beyond Good and Evil*
18; "herd animal" 59; *On the
Genealogy of Morals* 15–17, 28,
43; "The Over Soul" 48; *Thus
Spoke Zarathustra* 41, 44, 46

Oedipus 10

pain 3–4, 10, 12, 14, 29, 31, 33, 51–53,
63, 65, 67, 69
Peloponnesian War 7
philosophy 1–2, 7, 13, 23, 25, 36, 40, 46,
55, 58, 63–65
pity 17–18, 20
Plato 7, 23, 33, 40, 46, 53, 56, 59
psychoanalysis 8, 23, 42

psychology 1, 35, 38, 41–42, 58, 62
punishment 22, 30–32, 34–35, 37–38, 49

ressentiment 15, 18–19, 28, 36, 38–39, 45

sadism 33, 35, 39
Schopenhauer 7, 12
selflessness 17, 20, 24, 45
Shakespeare: *Cardenio* 31–32, 50; *The
Merchant of Venice* 32
Silenus 3–5, 7, 11, 50
Socrates 5, 22–23, 33, 52, 57
social life 9, 19, 30–32, 49

trauma 5, 8–11, 13, 24, 28–29, 36, 63
truth 3, 5–6, 12, 14, 17–18, 35, 39–40,
45, 50–51, 55–57, 59, 61;
absolute 64; and goodness 5;
gospel 58; objective 6, 13, 27,
58; terrible 47; traumatic 9

untruth 57

viciousness 64
violence 30–31, 34, 59

Wagner 36, 66
wisdom 3–5, 7, 11, 47, 50, 57

Zarathustra 46–54, 56

For Product Safety Concerns and Information please contact our EU
representative GPSR@taylorandfrancis.com
Taylor & Francis Verlag GmbH, Kaufingerstraße 24, 80331 München, Germany

www.ingramcontent.com/pod-product-compliance
Lightning Source LLC
Chambersburg PA
CBHW071058280326
41928CB00050B/2550